HAWAII'S POISONOUS PLANTS

HAWAII'S POISONOUS PLANTS

by

Roger E. Baldwin Ph. D.

Associate Professor of Biology
University of Hawaii, Hilo College

Plant Drawings
by
William Walker

Layout by
Hawaii Art Works

HILO
THE PETROGLYPH PRESS
STREET 96720
201 KINOOLE
HAWAII

Published and Distributed by
THE PETROGLYPH PRESS, LTD.
201 Kinoole Street
Hilo, Hawaii 96720

ISBN 0-912180-34-X

Published in the United States in 1979
First Printing - June 1979

TABLE OF CONTENTS

LIST OF PLANT DRAWINGS

PREFACE

In any work on poisonous plants an author has the problem of deciding which plants are to be considered poisonous. Any plant (or anything else) eaten in excess will make a person sick. Some persons are more susceptible than others to certain toxins. Some plants are only mildly toxic. Others vary in toxicity. Some plants are more poisonous when grown in some areas than in others. A plant may be poisonous only at certain times of the year. A plant may have both edible and poisonous parts. Some plants are poisonous to eat while others are dangerous to touch. Where can we draw the line?

For this book I have drawn the line by including those plants in Hawaii which have been implicated in poisonings or which are known to contain toxins which could easily become implicated. Various factors have been included in my decision: The toxicity of the plant, its prevalence in Hawaii, the likelihood of becoming poisoned, the frequency of past poisonings, here and elsewhere.

To help you, the reader, to know which plants to avoid and what to do when poisonings occur this book is organized into five chapters. The first chapter explains precautions and first aid procedures in general. The second chapter describes the plants which, because of their prevalence and high toxicity, are most likely to cause serious poisonings. The third chapter describes non-food plants which are less common or less toxic than those in the second chapter, but which are also likely to cause poisonings in Hawaii. The fourth chapter describes food plants which can cause poisonings. The fifth chapter describes the toxins found in plants in Hawaii.

This book has been written so that it can be understood by persons with no special knowledge of medicine or botany. It does contain technical terms but these are defined in the glossary (Appendix C). Definitions of chemical terms are not provided when they are readily available in encyclopedias.

For the physician or the reader with chemical training each toxin is categorized and named chemically if it is known. For the botanist Chapters II, III and IV and Appendix A are organized taxonomically according to the system of Cronquist and the Latin names are those listed as preferred names by St. John. (Both Cronquist's and St. John's books are listed in the references on p. 105). Appendix A lists many plants which I have felt are not important here, either because they are uncommon in Hawaii or of doubtful or trivial toxicity. References to other books which discuss them are provided for the reader interested in them. Since many references list plants under different names a list of alternate Latin names is provided in Appendix B.

It is hoped that you, the reader, will find the book both interesting and useful.

Roger E. Baldwin
June 1st, 1979

ACKNOWLEDGEMENTS

I wish to thank Dr. Frank Tabrah, who provided me with his unpublished data on *Wikstroemia pulcherrima.* I also wish to thank Dr. Harry L. Arnold Jr., who spent about two hours discussing the problem of plant-induced dermatitis, and Mr. Paul Weissich, who helped me obtain pictures of several plants in Foster Botanical Gardens.

Especial thanks are due to Dr. Rea Chittenden, who spent many hours helping me with this book. He provided much information from his experiences as Director of the Poison Information Center in Honolulu. He also critiqued and checked the medical accuracy of this book and provided the information about inducing vomiting provided in Chapter I.

Roger E. Baldwin
July 1, 1979

CHAPTER 1
GENERAL PRECAUTIONS AND FIRST AID

In Hawaii we are fortunate to have few poisonous plants. There are only nine genera which are both common and dangerously poisonous. Nevertheless, from time to time we do have poisonings, mostly among children and visitors. Unfortunately some of the dangerous plants are both beautiful and attractive to eat. It is to help you avoid them and enjoy the others that this book was written. Here are some guidelines:

1. Never experiment with unfamiliar plants -- with a few of them even a taste can kill you. Also some dangerously poisonous plants taste delicious (e.g., the coral plant), so taste is an unreliable criterion.

2. Become familiar with the common dangerous plants (described in Chapter II of this book) and the other poisonous plants (in Chapters III and IV).

3. Do not eat wild mushrooms or lichens unless you know the Hawaiian varieties. Some poisonous mushrooms in Hawaii may mislead a mainland expert.

4. Do not use sticks to skewer hot dogs or other food and do not use wood for campfires unless you know the wood is not poisonous.

5. Do not rely on unpleasant taste to deter small children. Until they are three years old their sense of taste is not fully developed and bitter taste is the last to develop. Small children will put anything into their mouths and they will not mind the flavor of some things which taste extremely unpleasant to older children and adults.

6. Do not consider a plant safe because animals eat it. Animals do *not* always know which plants are poison -- stock poisonings are commoner than human poisonings.

7. Do not assume a plant is safe just because it is not listed in this book. New plants are being brought into Hawaii all the time and it is certain that some of the new ones will be poisonous. Also we do not have information on all poisonous plants.

If you follow these guidelines you should have no difficulty with our Hawaiian plants -- the vast majority are safe to handle and enjoy.

TOXICITIES: In this book if the toxicity is known it is given in terms of grams or milligrams per kilogram of body weight. In other words, if a toxicity of 1.0 gm/kg body weight is stated, then for a seventy kilogram (150 pound) person the hazardous quantity is close to seventy grams. Seventy grams is about two and a half ounces or the size of a large plum. Because of the variety of ways the sources of information have determined toxicity some are stated as the minimum lethal dose (the smallest dose that killed), the LD_{50} (the dose which killed fifty per cent of the experimental animals) and the effective toxic dose (the minimum amount to produce toxic symptoms).

Another way of stating toxicity is by the terms, "moderately toxic," "highly toxic," and "dangerously toxic." The sources vary somewhat in the meaning of the terms, but they may be roughly interpreted as follows: "moderately toxic" means that a dose of five gm/kg body weight or more is necessary to cause symptoms (or sometimes to kill). "Highly toxic" means that the effective dose is between 0.1 and 5.0 gm/kg body weight. "Dangerously toxic" means that the effective dose is less than 0.1 gm/kg body weight, or it means that the plant is attractive to eat and a person is likely to receive a lethal dose if he tries to eat the plant at all. Also included among the "dangerously toxic" plants are those where sap in the eyes (by rubbing the eyes or other common activities) may threathen permanent blindness.

The toxicities given are frequently for animals because we often lack data on the amount necessary for human poisoning. It is prudent to assume that humans will be poisoned by a smaller relative dose than animals. At least, if we err it will be on the safe side. Also we should remember that it often takes less poison to affect a child, because he is smaller than an adult and because the toxins are frequently more toxic, weight for weight, with children than with adults.

FIRST AID

In all cases when plant poisoning is suspected and potentially serious enough for professional care *take a sample of the plant to the physician for identification*, even if you know the plant's name. Any sample will be helpful but it should include leaves, stems, flower and fruit, if possible.

IF THE PATIENT IS CONSCIOUS:

1. Always induce vomiting immediately if you suspect that a person has eaten a poisonous plant, even if there are no symptoms. Vomiting may be messy but it will not hurt a person in plant poisoning situations and it may save his life. *Do not wait for symptoms*, for that means that the poison has already caused damage. *There are no antidotes for most plant poisons.*
2. Consult a physician as soon as possible. Plant poisonings are frequently serious emergencies.
3. If you get poisonous plant material into the eyes, or if the eyes begin to smart, burn or itch after handling plants, wash the eyes with clear water for at least five minutes and go to a physician immediately. If possible have someone else take you.
4. If you get poisonous plant material into a wound or sore wash with clear water and go to a physician immediately.
5. If you get a rash, blisters or swelling of the skin wash the affected area with clear water for at least five minutes. If the symptoms persist see a physician for relief. Do not use ointments or grease -- the physician will only have to remove it and this may be painful.

SPECIAL COMMENT ABOUT DIARRHEA: Diarrhea is always potentially dangerous. However, if we were to include all of the plants which cause diarrhea the list would be very long indeed, for any plant eaten in excess will cause diarrhea unless it has substances which cause the opposite effect. The main danger with diarrhea is dehydration -- the body may lose so much liquid that the person may die. When diarrhea occurs, particularly with small children, a physician should be consulted if it is severe or if the symptoms persist for more than an hour or two.

SPECIAL COMMENTS ABOUT INDUCING VOMITING: For many of the plants you will find instructions to induce vomiting. You should attempt to do so, but sometimes a patient cannot vomit, no matter what you do. For such cases Dr. R. F. Chittenden of the Poison Information Center in Honolulu has graciously provided the following statement:

"Home remedies to produce emesis, such as warm salt water, with or without additions of household mustard, and with or without depression of the tongue or 'gagging' by applying pressure with an appropriate blunt object (smooth spoon handle) may or may not be of any value. They will often fail to produce the desired result, and plying the supposed victim repeatedly with salt water (of undetermined concentrations or strength) is a hazard, per se. Salt water poisoning has been produced sufficiently often to lead medical authorities to ask that such methods be prohibited, unless one can be certain of the limits or conditions which would prevent over-use or over-concentrations of the salt, or both. Actually in the latest pronouncements the salt water program is *abandoned*.

"It is possible in many households for persons to ask their physicians, in advance of an incident, his/her preference for producing vomiting -- which may well turn out to be keeping one ounce (or more) of *syrup* of ipecac in the household, and obtaining permission for its use from the physician or a poison information center as the occasion may arise. The usual dose, more or less in disregard of age/size, is one-half ounce (three teaspoons) by mouth, with the privilege of repeating in twenty minutes, for ONE ADDITIONAL DOSE in the same amount, if vomiting has not occurred.

"Vomiting occurs most easily on a full or partly full stomach, and administration of fluids after an emetic is encouraged."

One should note that in Dr. Chittenden's statement *syrup* of ipecac is specified. Other preparations of ipecac are more concentrated and ipecac is itself toxic, if taken in overdose.

IF THE PATIENT IS UNCONSCIOUS:

1. Take the patient to a physician immediately. Do *not* attempt to make him vomit and do not try to give him anything by mouth.

2. If the patient is not breathing make sure the mouth and throat are clear of obstructions. Apply artificial respiration.

Remember: take a sample of the plant to the physician for identification.

CHAPTER II

PLANTS DANGEROUSLY POISONOUS AND COMMON IN HAWAII

Argemone glauca (Nutt. ex Prain) Pope (pua-kala, Hawaiian poppy, Hawaiian pricklepoppy)

Very few native Hawaiian plants are poisonous; the pua-kala is one of them. It is found from sea level to above 3000 m (9000 ft.) in the wilder, open places of all the major Hawaiian Islands: in pastures, scrublands and dryland forests. It grows as a perennail herb to a height of from 0.3 to 1.5 m. (1-4 ft.). The tops frequently die back but new shoots grow from the fleshy roots. It is a pretty plant with blue-green leaves and white flowers but it has thorns on all parts except the roots. The leaves, up to 10 cm. (4 in.) long, are irregularly pinnately lobed with many thorns along the margins and veins. The whitish-green stems have many short, thin, extremely sharp spines. It is the only plant I know of with thorns among the stamens of the flowers. The flowers are white, typical poppies with yellow stamens. When open they are about 7 cm. (3 in.) across. The fruits are thorny capsules, 2-3 cm. long (about 1 in.), opening at the top. The seeds are about 1 mm. (1/25 in.), dark gray to black, and spherical. Because of its thorniness livestock avoid it.

Dr. Frank Tabrah of the University of Hawaii Medical School has studied the pua-kala. It contains alkaloids which have not been identified. It is likely that it has the same alkaloids as the Mexican poppy (*A. mexicana* L.), which has the isoquinoline alkaloids protopine, berberine, sanguinarine and dihydrosanguinarine. (K, 148) According to Dr. Tabrah, the whole plant is toxic with an LD_{50} of 0.75 gm/kg body weight. (personal communication) However, the toxins are concentrated in the

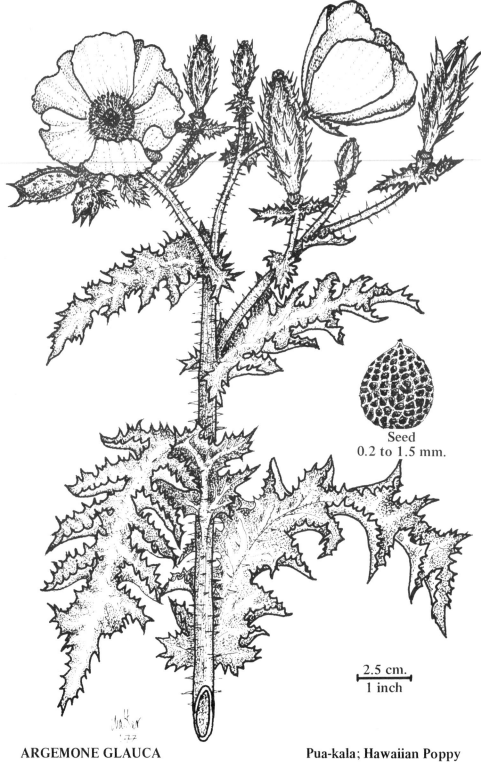

Seed
0.2 to 1.5 mm.

2.5 cm.
1 inch

ARGEMONE GLAUCA   **Pua-kala; Hawaiian Poppy**

orange-yellow sap which flows freely from damaged stems, leaves and roots. This suggests that the readily-obtained sap is much more toxic than the whole plant. Because the sap is quite bitter - I have tasted it myself, accidentally -- people are not likely to take toxic quantities, except small children (who cannot taste bitterness until about age three).

Marie Neal states that the Hawaiians formerly used bits of the plant to relieve symptoms of toothache, ulcers and neuralgia. (N, 367) It thus has local anesthetic properties. No cases of poisoning from pua-kala have been reported in recent years so its symptomology is unknown. Another species, *A. alba* Lestib., has frequently poisoned people in India and its symptoms are well-documented: vomiting, diarrhea, difficulty in seeing, fainting and coma. (Q,329; K,148) Pua-kala is likely to elicit similar symptoms. Dr. Tabrah states that pua-kala given to mice in small doses induces deep sleep.

FIRST AID: Induce vomiting if it has not already occurred. Do not attempt to check spontaneous vomiting and diarrhea. Take the patient to a physician. Keep the patient warm.

Abrus precatorius L. (jequirity bean, rosary pea, precatory bean, black-eyed Susan bean)

Many of us are familiar with the beautiful seeds used in jewelry. The seeds are locally called "black-eyed Susan" though they are not related to the garden flower of the same name. The plant is native to southern Asia. It likes hot, sunny areas. It is a perennial vine, climbing over other plants up to 5 m (15 ft). The leaves are pinnately compound, about 7 cm (3 in) long. The flowers look like tiny, white or pink or lavender sweet peas in racemes. The green pods in clusters ripen to black or dark brown, curling as they open to reveal four to eight seeds. The seeds are 1 cm (0.4 in) long 1/3 black and 2/3 scarlet. They are so uniform in size and weight that they have been used in India to measure the weights of jewelry and precious metals. The plant grows wild in the Puna and Kona districts of Hawaii island, where it is common. So far as I know the plant is not found elsewhere in Hawaii so people are most likely to encounter this plant as seeds in jewelry. Because I have seen such jewelry in many places I have included this among the common poisonous plants in Hawaii.

These seeds were recently an object of concern to the United States government when they were found in jewelry sold by mail order houses. The seeds are sufficiently poisonous that their sale in jewelry is banned by both federal and state laws. Concentrated in the seed coats is the phytotoxin, abrin. It is similiar, both chemically and in its action, to ricin (the toxin of *Ricinus*, pg. 20) and botulin (the toxin of botulism food poisoning). With a human lethal oral dose on 1.5 mg/kg body weight, the *seeds* are so toxic that one thoroughly chewed and swallowed may kill an adult. Absorbed through a cut or sore it is several hundred times more toxic; people have been seriously poisoned merely by pricking a finger while stringing the seeds into necklaces. Age does not weaken the toxin so even old seeds are poisonous. (Q, 358; K, 303; N, 81; A, 5)

Heat destroys the toxin, so the seeds are poisonous only when raw. Once when I was showing slides of this plant a student from Micronesia told me that he regularly ate them at his home. He said that they were cooked for a long time and served as we might serve pinto beans. The rest of the plant is only slightly toxic, if at all. The roots are edible when cooked, containing the flavoring agent of licorice, glycirrhizin. (Q, 358)

Unless a person gets the toxin into his eyes, a cut or a sore, where it causes immediate irritation, no symptoms appear for one or two days. When the seeds are

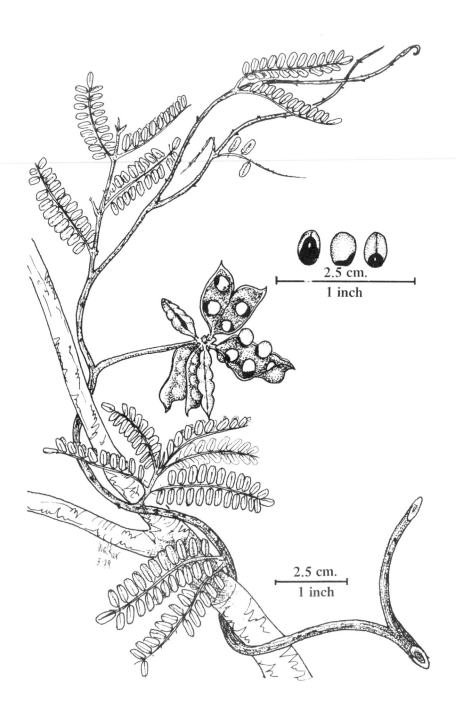

2.5 cm.
1 inch

2.5 cm.
1 inch

ABRUS PRECATORIUS   **Jequirity Bean**

eaten the first symptoms are likely to be irritation of the mouth and throat, followed by severe vomiting and diarrhea, often with bleeding. Later the person has poor coordination, difficulty in breathing and paralysis. Death is by respiratory failure. (K, 303; Q, 348)

FIRST AID: If you suspect that a person has eaten the seeds induce vomiting even if no symptoms have occurred. Wash suspected sores with water. Take the patient to a physician.

Jatropha spp.
Jatrophas are native to tropical America. The showy members of this genus are becoming quite common in Hawaii, especially the rose-flowered jatrophas. Jatrophas are shrubs or small trees grown in yards, hotel grounds, parks and graveyards. All have milky sap. (The uncommon species, *J curcas, J. gossypifolia* and *J. aconitifolia* are included in this chapter because they are similar in toxicology to the common ones).
J. integerrima Jacq., *J. hastata* Jacq. and *J. pandurifolia* Andr. are all called rose-flowered jatropha. St. John (S, 218) considers them all one species. There are certainly variety differences, at least, for the leaves vary in shape from oval to lanceolate and oblong, and some varieties have lobed or spurred leaves. Venation varies from pinnate to arcuate to palmate.

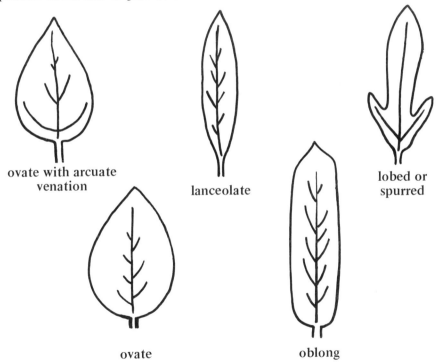

ovate with arcuate venation

lanceolate

lobed or spurred

ovate

oblong

The flowers are brilliant pink, with five petals, borne in clusters of about six flowers. The flowers are so distinctive that, knowing one of these plants, you will easily recognize the others. They grow as small trees with sparse foliage.

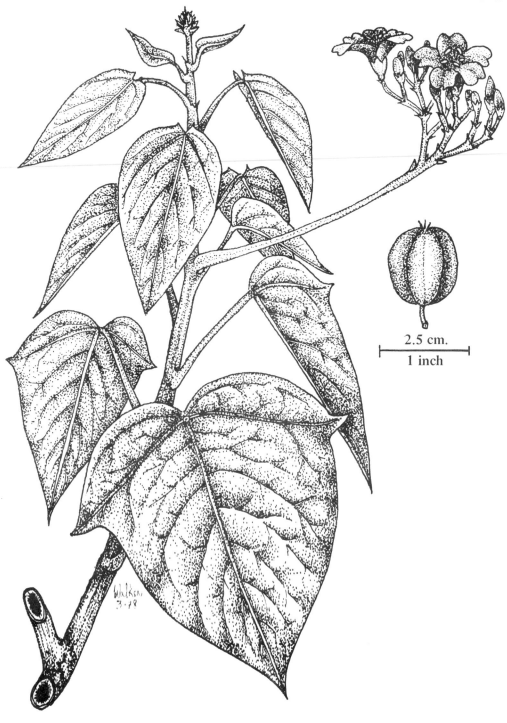

JATROPHA INTEGERRIMA   **Rose-flowered Jatropha**

2.5 cm.
1 inch

JATROPHA MULTIFIDA   **Coral Plant**

   J. multifida L. (coral plant) is named for its brilliant vermillion-pink clusters of flowers which look like branching coral. The flowers are tiny and the pedicels are as showy as the flowers themselves. It is a shrub or small tree, 1 to 3 meters (3 to 9 feet) tall. The leaves are about 30 centimeters (one foot) across, palmately deeply cleft into ten lobes.

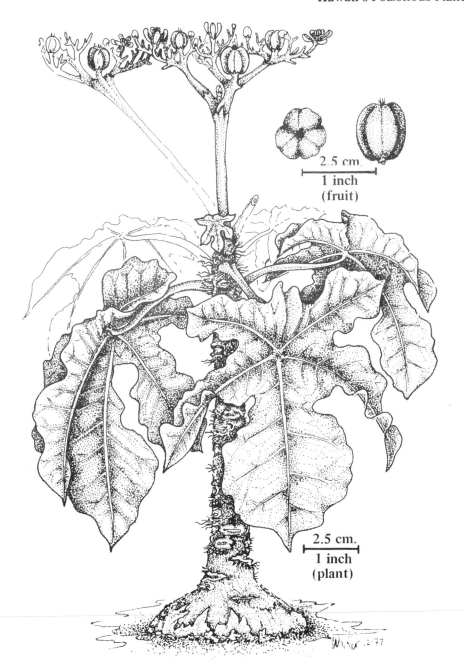

2.5 cm.
1 inch
(fruit)

2.5 cm.
1 inch
(plant)

JATROPHA PODAGRICA   Gout Plant

J. podagrica Hook. (gout plant) gets its name from the much-thickened base of the main stem. The flowers look much like those of *J. multifida*. It grows as a shrub, usually 30 to 60 centimeters (one to two feet) tall, but occasionally two meters (six feet) tall. The leaves are bluntly lobed, with three to five lobes, the whole leaf ten to twenty centimeters (four to eight inches) across.

J. aconitifolia Miller (survival plant) is the largest jatropha in Hawaii. It is fairly rare here, but it enjoyed a bit of popularity in the 1950's when the Watamull Foundation distributed them. This was when everyone was encouraged to build fall-out shelters. The idea was to have the trees growing near the shelters where occupants could momentarily leave the shelter, gather the leaves and return to the shelter to cook them. (Reginald Ho, personal communication) When raw the leaves cause severe gastroenteritis, but they are edible when cooked like spinach. (Paul Weissich and Dr. Rea Chittenden, personal communication)

The tree is four to five meters (twelve to fifteen feet) high, nicely rounded and with dense foliage. The leaves look like miniature papaya leaves fifteen to twenty centimeters (six to nine inches) across:

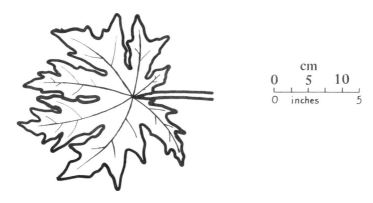

The plant has showy clusters of flowers the same size and shape as those of the coral plant, but intensely white. The floral clusters extend beyond the dark green foliage, making them quite showy.

J. curcas L. (physic nut) is a small tree. Its fruits are two centimeters (¾ inch) in diameter. They are green, opening as they ripen along three sutures, to yield three seeds. This plant is rare in Hawaii.

J. gossypifolia L. (cotton-leafed jatropha) is an herbaceous weed or somewhat woody shrub about one meter (three feet) high. The flower clusters, shaped like those of the coral plant, are dark purple and the leaves resemble those of the gout plant. It is rare in Hawaii.

Only *J. curcas* and *J. multifida* have been studied toxicologically. Since the symptoms of the others are similar to those of these plants it is likely that they have similar poisons. *J. curcas* has several substances which may be toxic but two of them are the substances mainly responsible for the symptoms. Most toxic is the albuminold phytotoxin, curcin, which is similar to the toxins of *Abrus* (p. 13) and *Ricinus* (p. 20). The seeds also contain purgative oil more potent than castor oil but not as drastic as croton oil, with concentrations as high as fifty per cent of the seeds' weight. (K, 190; Q, 512) (Incidently the "crotons" so commonly grown in Hawaii are not true crotons and they do not contain croton oil or any other toxic substance, as far as I can determine from the literature.) The toxicity of jatrophas varies considerably from plant to plant, even within a species. Two or three seeds of *J. curcas* or *J. multifida* may cause severe symptoms, so the plant can be about as toxic as *Ricinus*. Some cases have required more of the plant to cause symptoms and a few instances have been reported of *J. curcas* plants which are nontoxic. Unfortunately the fruits are delicious to taste, so persons testing the fruit are likely to consume hazardous amounts. (A,11; K, 190; Q,512; O, 55; H, 117)

Jatrophas initially cause a burning sensation in the mouth and throat. Later symptoms are vomiting, diarrhea with blood, and coma. Symptoms may occur within minutes but they are more likely to be delayed several hours. (K, 190)

FIRST AID: Induce vomiting if it has not already occurred. Take the patient to a physician. Do not wait for symptoms to occur.

Ricinus communis L. (castor bean)

Castor beans are native to Africa but they grow throughout the tropics and subtropics of the world. They are common in Hawaii, both wild and in yards, up to elevations of 1000 meters (3000 feet) above sea level. The plant is a coarse, sprawling bush or small tree. It has no central stem, sending out many branches. They are only slightly if at all woody and except at the base they are hollow. The leaves, usually about thirty centimeters (one foot) across, may vary in width from ten to seventy centimeters (four to thirty inches). The leaves are deeply cleft, so they appear star-shaped, with five to eleven points. Separate male and female flowers occur on the same plant in terminal racemes. The tiny male flowers are pale yellow. The female flowers have reddish sepals, but the most conspicuous part is the green pistil which swells into a round fruit covered with soft bristles. The fruit is first green, ripening to a dark brown capsule. The capsule contains usually five bean-shaped seeds, mottled purplish or brownish gray, about one centimeter (one half inch) long.

Castor beans are the source of the laxative, castor oil. However, the seeds are dangerous because of another poison, the phytotoxin ricin. The rest of the plant may be somewhat poisonous, but the seeds have the highest concentrations of the toxin. Ricin is similar chemically and toxicologically to abrin (See *Abrus*, p. 13). The main difference in the action of the two poisons is that abrin is highly irritating while ricin is not. Thus castor beans do not cause inflammation of eyes, mouth and wounds like jequirity beans do. (K, 194; Q, 529) Juliette Wentworth of Hilo, who had the unfortunate experience of eating castor beans, tells me that they are not unpleasant tasting. One castor bean, when eaten, causes purging. Four seeds can kill a person and eight almost certainly will. Like abrin, ricin is absorbed more readily through wounds and sores than when eaten. People can be poisoned by pricking their fingers while stringing jewelry. (K, 194; Q, 529) Like jequirity beans the castor beans may not be used legally in jewelry.

Ricin is considerably more toxic than abrin. The minimum lethal dose of ricin is 0.0001 mg/kg body weight subcutaneously and 0.01 mg/kg orally. However, jequirity beans are more toxic than castor beans, since they have more toxin. (K,194; K, 303)

Symptoms of castor bean poisoning are twofold. A short time after eating them there is the characteristic purging from castor oil. After one or two days the person has the symptoms of ricin poisoning: severe diarrhea and vomiting, excessive thirst, prostration, dullness of vision and convulsions.

FIRST AID: Induce vomiting immediately if ingestion is even suspected. Wash suspected wounds with water. Take the patient to a physician. Do not wait for symptoms to occur.

2.5 cm.
1 inch

fruit
flowers

1 cm.
0.4 inch
(seeds)

2.5 cm.
1 inch
(plant)

Walter
1-78

RICINUS COMMUNIS

Castor Bean

togoma

2.5 cm.
1 inch
(plant)

NERIUM INDICUM   Oleander (single blossom variety)

NERIUM INDICUM

Oleander (double blossom variety)

2.5 cm.

1 inch

Nerium indicum Miller and *N. oleander* L. (oleander)

Oleander is from southern Europe and the Middle East. The trees may grow in excess of 7 m (20 ft) but they are usually pruned to lower heights. The leaves are dark green, lanceolate, 10 to 20 cm (4 - 8 in.) long. Single flowers are five-petaled and there are double varieties. The flowers are white, pink or red, in clusters, the individual flowers usually 5 cm (2 in.) across. The fruits grow as pairs of green, slender, pod-like capsules 10-15 cm (4-6 in.) long. It is by far the commonest tree in Honolulu. It is grown in yards and parks and in medial strips of highways throughout the islands, just as it is in California. It is not hard to understand its popularity. It grows easily in sunny places and needs no more watering and fertilizing than the lawn it is growing in. Its slender stems are easily pruned. Few pests attack it. It is a clean tree, for it has few fruits and its flowers disintegrate rapidly after they fall, making it unnecessary to rake them up. In short it has everything one can desire in an ornamental tree except one: it is deadly.

The poisons, named oleandrin, oleandroside and neriin, are cardiac glycosides. The whole plant is extremely toxic. A single leaf can kill an adult and people have been killed by meat roasted over campfires on oleander sticks. (K, 264; Q, 729; A, 13) With such popularity and high toxicity, the only reason I can think of that few people are poisoned is that everybody knows that oleanders are poisonous.

Oleander symptoms appear soon after the plant is eaten: nausea, vomiting, abdominal pain and dizziness. The pulse slows and becomes irregular. The pupils dilate and the patient becomes drowsy. Diarrhea with bleeding sometimes occurs. Death is by respiratory and cardiac failure, the heart stopping in systolic contraction ("in systole"). (See *Digitalis*,(p. 62)(K, 264; Q, 729)

FIRST AID: Induce vomiting if it has not already started. Do not attempt to check spontaneous vomiting and diarrhea. Take the patient to a physician. Speed is essential.

Thevetia peruviana (Pers.) K. Schum, and *T. thevetioides* (HBK) K. Schum. (be-still tree, yellow oleander)

T. peruviana comes from South America. In Hawaii it is an ornamental in parks and yards of the lowlands. It is a handsome tree, up to 4 m (12 ft) tall, forming a well-rounded shape. It has dark, shiny leaves 7-15 cm (3 to 6 in) long and about 6 mm (¼ in) wide. The leaves roll under at the margins. The bright yellow, funnel-shaped flowers grow in terminal clusters. (There is also a salmon-pink variety.) The flowers are somewhat fragrant, with five petal lobes cleft about halfway down. The fruit is green to black, about 3 cm (1.2 in) across and nearly spherical, but with three rounded corners. It contains two black seeds which nearly fill the fruit. *T. thevetiodes* is similar, but with larger flowers. The fruits look as though they should be good to eat, but they are extremely toxic. It is from eating the fruits that most poisonings occur.

The poison is thevetin, a cardiac glycoside. All parts of the plant are highly poisonous, one seed being sufficient to kill a child. (A, 9; K, 266; Q, 740)

Thevetin symptoms occur within minutes after a person eats the plant. Although the poison is similar to that of Digitalis (p. 62) the symptoms are somewhat different. Thevetin causes high blood pressure which continues for a long time. Vomiting is frequent. The heartbeat is slow and irregular and suddenly stops in systolic contraction ("in systole"). (Q, 740)

FIRST AID: Induce vomiting if it has not already started. Do not attempt to check spontaneous vomiting. Take the patient to a physician. Speed is essential.

THEVETIA PERUVIANA   **Be-still tree**

2.5 cm
1 inch

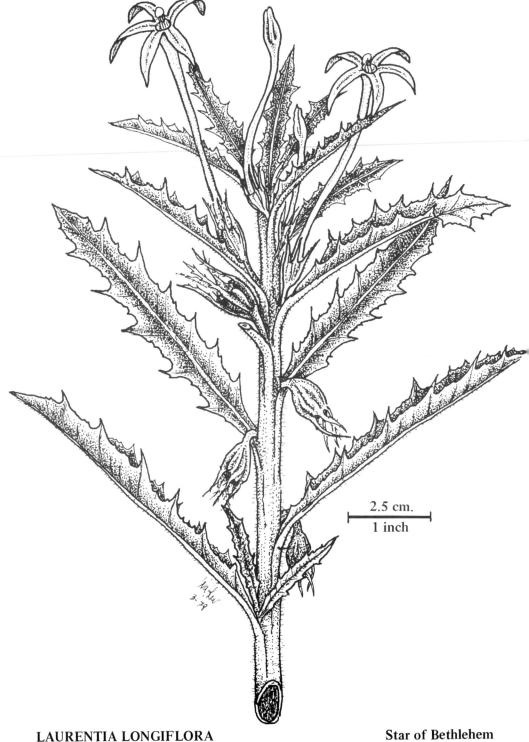

LAURENTIA LONGIFLORA   **Star of Bethlehem**

Laurentia longiflora (L.) Engl. (star of Bethlehem)

The plant, locally called "star of Bethlehem," is a weed and not the handsome garden plant (*Ornithogalum* spp.) of the same common name. It comes from tropical America. It is a common roadside weed in Hilo and Puna districts of Hawaii island, and it is less common elsewhere in Hawaii. It grows about 30 cm (one foot) high, occasionally as high as 50 centimeters (twenty inches). It has narrow, dark-green, irregularly pinnate-lobed leaves, 7 to 15 centimeters (two to six inches) long. The lobes and leaf tips come to points, but there are no thorns. The flowers, borne singly at the leaf axils, are intensely white, contrasting with the dark green of the leaves. Each flower has a narrow corolla tube up to eight centimeters (three inches) long, abruptly ending with five petal lobes, each about one centimeter long (½ inch). The fruit is a soft, ridged capsule about one centimeter (½ inch) long.

Laurentia contains at least two pyridine alkaloids: lobeline and nicotine. The former is mainly responsible for the symptoms and the latter is the familiar alkaloid in tobacco. All parts of the plant are toxic.

From personal experience I can say that this plant is highly irritant, even to touch. Once I was helping a student take pictures of a plant and I had only lightly touched it. A friend of mine came by and offered me a handful of pretzels. I ate a few pretzels and immediately my mouth had sensations of burning, numbness and "pins-and-needles." I immediately washed out my mouth with water but it was an hour before the symptoms disappeared. Another time, not knowing that lobeline can be absored through intact skin, I pulled up some plants bare-handed, and again the burning, "pins-and-needles" symptoms appeared, this time in the hands.

The plant is also dangerous because small amounts of the sap in the eye (e.g. from rubbing the eyes after handling the plant) can cause blindness. In larger doses both lobeline and nicotine cause vomiting, paralysis of the voluntary muscles, rapid and feeble heartbeat and irregular respiration. Trembling may occur. (A, 45; D1, fam 339; N, 818; Q, 953; PT, 522; Dr, 111) Because of its highly irritant properties and because toxic amounts can be absorbed through intact skin the plant should not be handled. Use tools in eradication (i.e., do not pull them up by hand) and wash the tools thoroughly when finished.

FIRST AID: If you get the sap onto your skin or into your eyes, mouth or a cut, wash thoroughly with cold water for at least five minutes. With eye contact see a physician without delay. If taken internally induce vomiting immediately and take the person to a physician. Speed is essential.

Datura spp. (datura, angel's trumpet, jimson weed, kīkānia haole, lāʻau-hānō).

D. arborea L. and *D. candida* (Pers.) Pasq. are both called "angel's trumpet." They are native to South America. Both grow in Hawaii, though *D. candida* is more common here. This species is an ornamental shrub or tree in yards, parks and gardens. It grows as high as five meters (fifteen feet), but more often two to three meters (six to nine feet) high. The stems are woody but weak and often-branched. It has downy ovate leaves pointed at the tip. The flowers are usually white, though I have seen pale salmon-pink ones also. The flowers are pendulous. The showy, thirty cm. (one foot) long, trumpet-shaped corolla emerges from a green calyx tube one-third as long. The corolla has five lobes, each pointed at the tip. The plant seldom fruits, but when it does the fruit is a smooth, ovoid capsule about six centimeters (two to three inches) long. *D. arborea*, according to Marie Neal (N, 748), differs mainly in having a calyx tube as long as the throat of the corolla.

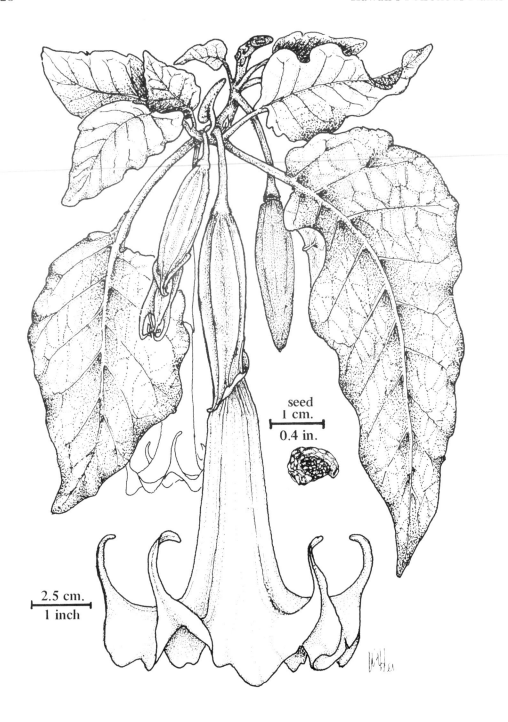

seed
1 cm.
0.4 in.

2.5 cm.
1 inch

DATURA CANDIDA   **Angel's Trumpet**

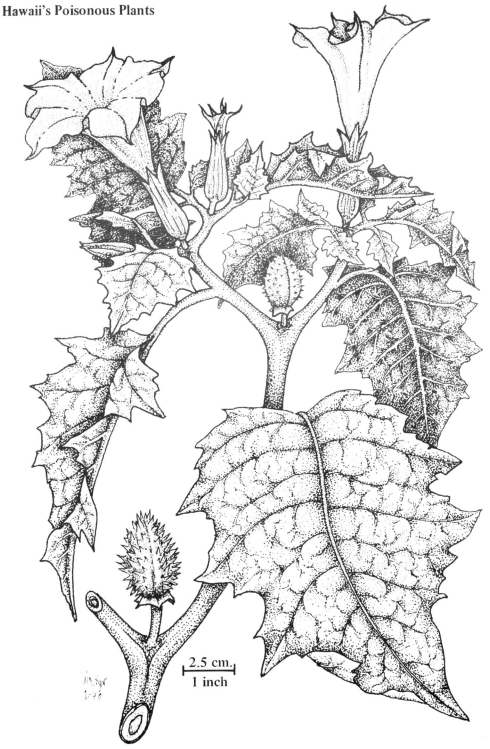

2.5 cm.
1 inch

DATURA STRAMONIUM   Jimson Weed

D. stramonium L. (jimson weed, Jamestown weed, kīkānia-haole) is from southern Asia. It is a fairly common roadside and pasture weed in Hawaii. It grows 1 to 1.6 meters (three to five feet) high, with flowers similar to the angel's trumpet, but smaller (ten centimeters or four inches long), and white to purple in color. The flowers are erect. The leaves, ovate to lanceolate, have coarse-dentate margins. The fruit is a thorny capsule five centimeters (two inches) long.

D. metel L. (garden datura, cornucopia) is a native of southeastern Asia and Indonesia. It is not very common in Hawaii, but it is occasionally found both wild and in gardens. It is included in this chapter because it is similar both toxicologically and biologically to the other species of *Datura*. It grows as an herb up to 1.6 meters (five feet) high. The leaves are similar to those of jimson weed except that the margins are wavy, rather than dentate. The flowers are about fifteen centimeters (seven inches) long, somewhat smaller than angel's trumpet. The flowers appear like three nested yellow trumpets. The fruit is a thorny, globose capsule about three centimeters (a little over an inch) in diameter.

All species of *Datura* contain the tropane alkaloids atropine, hyoscyamine and scopolamine. They are dangerous to handle, mainly because sap rubbed into the eyes can cause permanent blindness and injury to the eyes. (K, 278) When I was a child two neighbor children handled the flowers and then rubbed their eyes. The pupils dilated and the children had to wear dark glasses for several days until their eyes recovered.

Used in carefully controlled doses atropine is a very useful drug. It is used in eye examinations to dilate the pupils. It is also administered before surgery to reduce salivation and to relax the patient. On the other hand, atropine is extremely dangerous to those threatened with glaucoma, a serious eye disease.

Besides the eye symptoms, *Datura,* is toxic when taken internally. It causes thirst (due to cessation of saliva secretion), dry mouth and pupil dilation. In larger doses it gives a person headache, hallucinations, fever, nausea, rapid heartbeat and delirium. Blood pressure may drop severely. It is interesting that *Datura* and *Cestrum* (p. 56) have the same or similar toxins but cause different symptoms. (A, 17; H, 137; K, 278).

FIRST AID: If sap gets into the eyes wash with clear water for at least five minutes. If taken internally induce vomiting. Take the patient to a physician immediately. Speed is essential.

Dieffenbachia spp. (dumbcane)

The native habitat of *Dieffenbachia* is Central and South America. In Hawaii it is grown as an ornamental in and around houses, in parks and hotels. It likes semi-shady areas with plenty of moisture.

There are about twenty five species of *Dieffenbachia* but they are similar in appearance. They all have glossy leaves, sometimes uniformly green but more commonly variegated green and white. The leaves grow alternately along an upright, cane-like stem. The plants are usually one to two meters (three to six feet) high. The commonest species here is *D. sequine* (Jacq.) Schott. This species has leaves 35 to 75 centimeters (14 to 30 inches) long, more or less oblong in shape with petioles up to forty centimeters (sixteen inches) long. The fruits are clusters of orange or red berries in a large bract.

Another genus, *Aglaonema*, overlaps with *Dieffenbachia* in general appearance. (i.e., there is considerable variation in the appearance of both genera, and some species of *Aglaonema* look very similar to some species of *Dieffenbachia.*) *Aglaonema* is not as toxic as *Dieffenbachia* but both have calcium oxalate crystals which alone can cause irritation of the mouth and throat. It would be well to take the same care

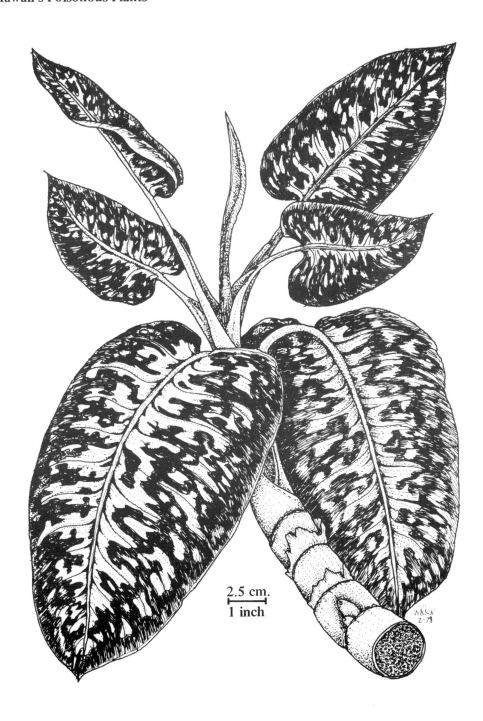

DIEFFENBACHIA sp.   Dumbcane

with both genera because the two can be easily confused and because both are toxic.

Dieffenbachia is considerably more toxic than the calcium oxalate crystals alone can account for. It appears that it also has some extremely toxic proteins, but the nature of these proteins is not fully known. (K, 473; H, 49)

Some people are more sensitive to these plants than others. Some people get irritation and edema of the skin from merely handling the intact plants. This may be an allergic reaction but it is fairly common. However, everyone has a painful reaction if he puts any part of the plant into his mouth. (Marie Neal claims that the fruits are non-toxic) (N, 151). There is immediate, excruciating burning and tingling of the mouth and throat. Salivation increases. Tissues of the mouth and throat become seriously irritated and edematous. This irritation may extend into the pharynx and vocal cords, making the person unable to vocalize. This, with the swelling of the tongue, prevents the person from speaking (hence the name, "dumbcane"). Occasionally the edema of the throat may be so severe as to cause choking, and this is why the plant is dangerous. The edema is slow to disappear, lasting as long as a week. (K, 473; H, 49)

FIRST AID: Wash the mouth and throat (or any affected part) with water or cold tea. It often helps to suck ice cubes, but spit out the liquid. If the person has swallowed a piece of the plant induce vomiting immediately. Take the patient to a physician. Because of the danger of choking, speed is essential.

CHAPTER III:
POISONOUS NON-FOOD PLANTS IN HAWAII

Anemone hupehensis Lem. & Lem. f. (Japanese anemone)

This plant is native to China. It is grown in gardens of the cooler parts of the Hawaiian Islands, and around Kilauea Volcano it grows wild in the wet forests. It is a perennial herb which grows up to 1.5 meters (four feet) high. The basal leaves are compound with three asymmetrically ovate leaflets. The leaves have long petioles. The upper leaves are simple bracts surrounding the base of the flower stalk. The flowers bloom in the fall and are usually white, but occasionally pink, red or purple. Each flower has six to nine showy sepals. (There are no petals.) As the flower ripens the central ball breaks open to release seeds with attached hairs which allow them to float in the wind.

Anemones contain an oil, ranunculin, which is itself harmless, but which readily breaks down in the human digestive tract into an irritant and vesicant oil, protoanemonin. Symptoms include salivation, diarrhea, abdominal pain, depression and convulsions. (K, 140)

FIRST AID: Induce vomiting if it has not occurred spontaneously. Do not attempt to check spontaneous vomiting and diarrhea. See a physician if the symptoms are severe or persistent.

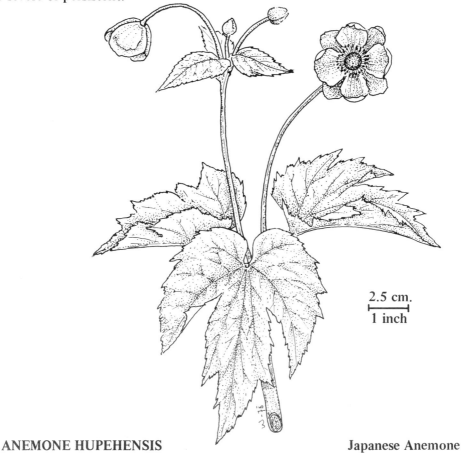

2.5 cm.
⊢———⊣
1 inch

ANEMONE HUPEHENSIS   Japanese Anemone

Delphinium spp. (delphinium, larkspur)

Delphiniums are garden flowers native to Europe and North America. They grow in gardens at Kilauea Volcano and Waimea on Hawaii island and in the Kula district on Maui. They grow up to 1.6 meters (five feet) high. The most conspicuous part of the plant is the long spike, crowded with many blue, pink or white flowers. The flowers are curiously shaped. The five petaloid sepals are showy and one has a spur which encloses a similar spur from the single petal. In Hawaii these flowers are most frequently encountered in cut arrangements from florist shops.

Delphiniums contain several polycyclic diterpene alkaloids, particularly delphinine, lycoctonine and aconitine. The whole plant is toxic but the seeds are the most toxic part. Toxicity decreases as the plant matures. Toxicity varies between specimens but all delphiniums should be considered poisonous. (ACS, 473; ACS, 533; H, 56; K, 131)

Eating of delphiniums causes vomiting and diarrhea. Pulse becomes rapid and there is involuntary muscular twitching, weakness and both muscular and respiratory paralysis. Survivors become constipated as they recover. (K, 131)

FIRST AID: If the patient is conscious induce vomiting if it has not already occurred. Do not attempt to check spontaneous vomiting and diarrhea. See a physician if the symptoms persist or if the patient is unconscious. Do not attempt to induce vomiting if the patient is unconscious.

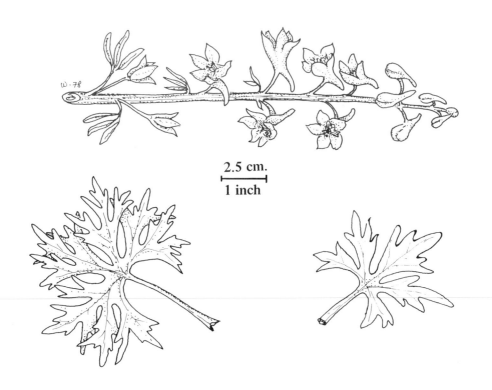

2.5 cm.

1 inch

DELPHINIUM sp.   **Larkspur**

Papaver somniferum L. (opium poppy) is native to Europe and the Middle East. People frequently have the mistaken idea that opium poppies grow only in restricted environments, but they are rare in the United States only because growing them is illegal. Before the Harrison Narcotics Act of 1914 was passed opium poppies were common in Hawaii and throughout the United States. They contain morphine, codeine and related isoquinoline alkaloids.

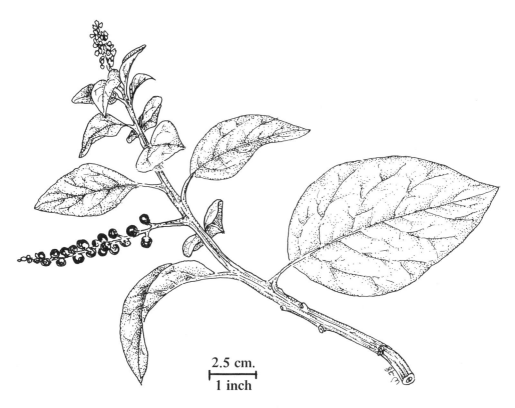

2.5 cm.
1 inch

PHYTOLACCA SANDWICENSIS   Pōpolo-ku-mai

Phytolacca spp. (pokeberry, pōpolo-ku-mai)
    Three species of *Phytolacca* grow in Hawaii. A native Hawaiian species, *P. sandwicensis* Endl. (pōpolo-ku-mai), is a rough, herbaceous or somewhat woody, perennial which grows wild in the open rainforests of Hawaii, Maui, Molokai, Oahu and Kauai. It is not uncommon on the outer islands, but it is extremely rare on Oahu, according to Degener. (D1, fam 115) The plant grows from 80 to 140 centimeters (two to four feet) high, usually erect but occasionally sprawling or trailing. The leaves, six to fifteen centimeters (two to six inches) long, are elliptic to oval, alternately arranged along the stem. The leaves are smooth to somewhat hairy. The small flowers are white to deep pink in narrow, nearly erect racemes. This plant, like other species of *Phytolacca,* has two characteristics which make it distinctive. One is the pigmented older stems, in this species brown to bright purple. The other is the arrangement of the dark purple, juicy berries in racemes. (This is sufficiently distinc-

tive that one should be cautious about eating any berries growing in racemes.)

Two other species of *Phytolacca* are also found in Hawaii. *P. octandra* L. (southern pokeberry) is another rough herbaceous plant, similar to pōpolo-ku-mai, but with narrower leaves. It also has dark purple fruits in racemes, and it usually has reddish stems. It is native to Mexico. Rare in Hawaii is the large tree, *P. dioica* L. (ombu, bella sombra), which is occasionally found in parks.

The species found here in Hawaii have not been studied for their toxicity, but the related species, *P. americana* L. (pokeberry) has been studied. (It does not occur in Hawaii.) Several poisons have been reported in *P. americana* but none have been verified. It is quite poisonous and as few as ten berries can cause severe symptoms. The root is the most toxic part, but any part of the plant may be poisonous. Most human poisonings have involved eating raw berries or young shoots. (Both berries and leaves are edible when properly cooked.) (H, 71; K, 225)

Immediately after eating pokeberry a person feels a burning sensation in the mouth. About two hours later this is followed by cramps, vomiting and diarrhea, difficulty in breathing, visual disturbances, weakness and possibly convulsions. (K, 225; H, 71)

FIRST AID: Induce vomiting if it has not already occurred. Do not attempt to stop spontaneous vomiting and diarrhea. Consult a physician.

Rivinia humilis L. (rouge plant, coral berry)

Rouge plant is native to both North and South America. It is occasionally grown in gardens and yards in Honolulu, but it is not common in Hawaii. It is closely related to *Phytolacca* (above) and fairly similar to it. The fruits are red berries in racemes. Symptoms and first aid are the same as those for *Phytolacca*. (A, 51)

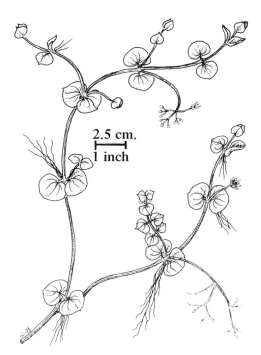

2.5 cm.
1 inch

DRYMARIA CORDATA   Pipili

Drymaria cordata (L.) Willd. (drymary, pipili)
    This grows as a weak-stemmed weed in the wetter, shady parts of yards and gardens. The creeping stems may be as long as 40 centimeters (16 inches) with pairs of orbicular to cordate leaves every two centimeters (¾ inch). It is particularly annoying because its tiny greenish fruits stick to clothing and to pets and are hard to remove. It may cause diarrhea and vomiting if eaten, but this is not likely, except with small children, because it is extremely bitter. The lethal dose of a related species *(D. pachyphylla* Woot. & Standl., not found here) to cattle and sheep is five grams per kilogram of body weight. (K, 247)

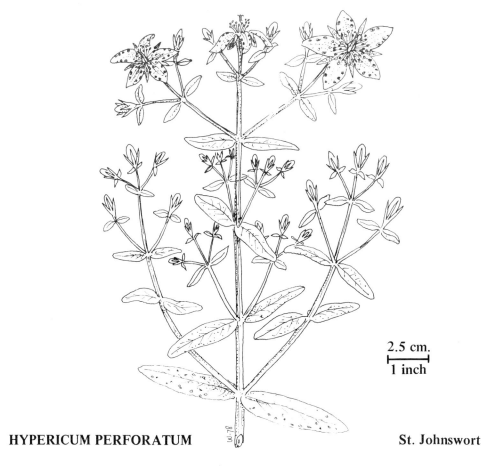

2.5 cm.
1 inch

HYPERICUM PERFORATUM   St. Johnswort

Hypericum perforatum L. (St. Johnswort, Klamath weed)
    St. Johnswort comes from Europe. It is an herbaceous to somewhat woody pasture weed, thirty to a hundred centimeters (one to three feet) tall, with many opposite-arranged lateral stems. The narrow leaves are also opposite, one to three centimeters (1/3 to one inch) long. There are five sepals, five petals and many stamens. The ovary has three spreading styles.
    St. Johnswort is toxic because of a primary photosensitizer, hypericin. This substance is absorbed unchanged by the digestive tract and then carried to the skin and the retina, where it increases the light-absorbing capability of the skin and eyes. (K, 171; A, 41)

The plant has seldom, if ever, been implicated in human poisonings. Among stock the symptoms are those of sunburn and heatstroke: dermatitis with peeling; rapid heartbeat and breathing, elevated temperature, convulsions. The symptoms do not occur in animals protected from sunlight. Light-colored animals are more seriously affected than dark ones and spotted animals frequently show symptoms of dermatitis only in the light-colored areas. (K, 171)

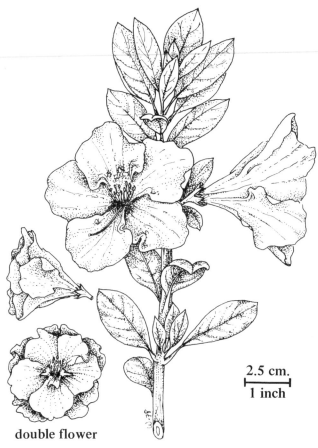

2.5 cm.
1 inch

double flower

RHODODENDRON INDICUM   Azalea

Rhododendron indicum (L.) Sweet (azalea)
    Azaleas (in Hawaii) are native to Japan. They are grown in yards, gardens and parks throughout Hawaii. They grow well at both higher and lower elevations and in both wet and dry areas. They are usually described as small bushes but some in my front yard are over two and a half meters (seven feet) high. The leaves are lanceolate, up to five centimeters (two inches) long, alternately arranged on the stem, though the short internodes often make them appear clustered at the stem tips. There are many horticultural varieties of this plant, both single- and double-flowered forms. The single-flowered varieties have five showy petals in a somewhat funnel-shape. Color varies from white through pink to red and purple and there are some with variegated flowers. The fruit is an ovoid capsule.

Azaleas contain the resin andromedotoxin. Toxicity varies considerably from plant to plant but they should always be considered poisonous. Poisoning in humans has occurred mostly when children have sucked the flowers for nectar. The flowers are safe to handle and to use in bouquets. (K, 225; H, 122)

Early symptoms are watering of the eyes and mouth. The person complains of loss of energy and tiredness. Later he vomits and his blood pressure drops. In severe cases (highly unlikely) the patient has poor coordination, convulsions and progressive paralysis of the limbs. (H, 122)

FIRST AID: Induce vomiting and take the patient to a physician.

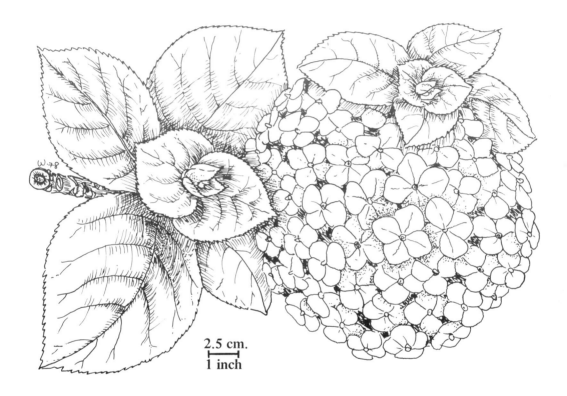

2.5 cm.
1 inch

HYDRANGEA MACROPHYLLA   Hydrangea

Hydrangea macrophylla Ser. (hydrangea)

Hydrangeas are native to eastern Asia. In Hawaii they are a common yard and garden shrub, often pruned into hedges. They grow at any elevation but they are especially popular in cooler areas. The plant grows from one to four meters (three to twelve feet) high. The leaves are opposite in arrangement, eight to twenty centimeters (three to eight inches) long, ovate with pointed tips and with coarsely dentate margins. The large, showy heads of flowers have the interesting feature of being alterable in color, depending upon the nutrients in the soil. Liming the soil favors pink flowers, while untreated Hawaiian soil grows blue-flowered plants. White varieties exist also.

I can find no reference confirming human poisonings from hydrangeas, but stock poisonings have occurred and the plant is known to contain the cyanogenic glycoside, amygdalin. (K, 370; H, 78) See *Manihot* for symptoms. (p. 67)

FIRST AID: Induce vomiting if it has not occurred spontaneously. Administer oxygen if it is available. Take the patient to a physician. Speed is essential, for cyanide is a rapid killer.

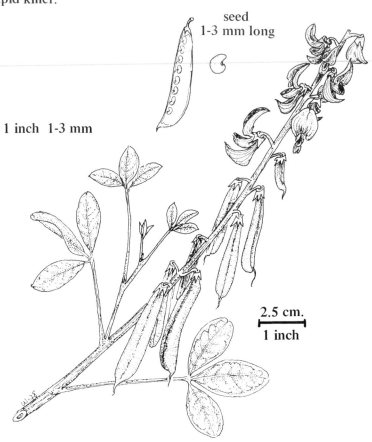

seed
1-3 mm long

1 inch 1-3 mm

2.5 cm.
1 inch

CROTALARIA MUCRONATA   **Rattle Pod**

Crotalaria spp. (rattle pod, rattle box)

Crotalaria is a large genus of herbaceous plants from all over the world. In Hawaii they grow along roadsides, in pastures and open fields. They have racemes of yellow flowers shaped like sweet peas. They vary in height between 0.3 and one meter (one to three feet). These plants are attractive to children because the seeds come loose and rattle inside the unopen, inflated pods. .

The poison of *Crotalaria* is the pyrrolizidine alkaloid, monocrotaline. The toxicity of the plant to hogs varies from species to species from nontoxic to a toxicity of 0.1 gm/kg of body weight. The toxicity in humans has not been determined but people have been poisoned by this plant. All parts of the plant are toxic, but the seeds are the most poisonous. (K, 314; ACS, 473; 533) Luckily they are attractive mainly as rattles and are seldom eaten, but children should be cautioned not to eat them. They are safe to handle.

The symptoms are frequently very slow in appearing. They may appear within a few days but there have been cases where stock showed symptoms six months after the last time they had access to *Crotalaria*. (K, 314) The toxin damages the liver. Human poisonings are rare and symptomology is obscure. Symptoms in stock primarily involve the lower intestinal tract: diarrhea, with or without bleeding, and painful bowel movements. Bleeding sometimes extends to the entire gastrointestinal tract and nasal passages. (K, 314)

FIRST AID: If a person has eaten *Crotalaria*, particularly the seeds, induce vomiting. Consult a physician even if the person seems normal. Do not wait for symptoms. They are slow in coming, but when they occur severe liver damage has already occurred.

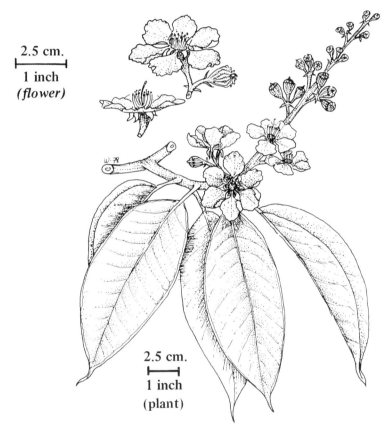

2.5 cm.

1 inch
(flower)

2.5 cm.

1 inch
(plant)

LAGERSTROEMIA INDICA   Queen Flower, Crape Myrtle

Lagerstroemia indica L. (Queen flower) and *L. speciosa* (L.) Pers. (crape myrtle)

These plants are native to China, India, southeastern Asia and Indonesia. *L. indica* is a three-meter (nine-foot) shrub and *L. speciosa* is a large tree. The latter is quite common in Hawaii as a shade tree and ornamental. In February the leaves turn brilliant red and yellow and fall off -- real "autumn leaves." Then the pink, new foliage starts to grow and later turns green. The new leaves have barely turned green in May when the panicles of bright lavender flowers burst into bloom all over the tree. **The tree remains in bloom often through July. The rest of the year the plant is a** handsome tree, up to twenty meters (sixty feet) high, with medium green foliage. The leaves are oval, three to six centimeters (one to two inches) long. The plant is locally called "kāhili flower" because the panicles of flowers resemble the feathered staffs of the Hawaiians. Another quite different plant, *Grevillea banksii* (p. 37) is also called "kāhili flower."

Neither of the *lagerstroemias* has been reported to cause poisoning in humans, but they are known to contain a substance which causes hypoglycemia (lowered blood sugar). A toxic dose of the leaves (to rabbits) is one gram per kg. body weight (Q, 639).

FIRST AID: Induce vomiting and take the patient to a physician.

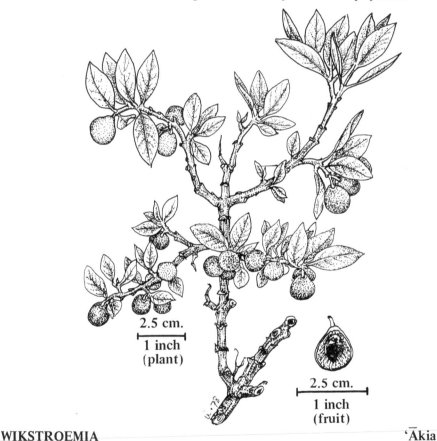

2.5 cm.
1 inch
(plant)

2.5 cm.
1 inch
(fruit)

WIKSTROEMIA   'Ākia

Wikstroemia spp. ('ākia, false 'ōhelo)
This genus includes many native species and every major Hawaiian island has several endemic species. They vary somewhat, but all are woody shrubs with tough, smooth bark. The leaves are small and ovate, and with most species they are bluish green in color. The flowers are tiny (only a few millimeters long), tubular, four-parted and yellow. The fruits are yellow, orange or red ovoid drupes. With most species the fruits are smaller than one centimeter (0.4 inch), though one species (*W. pulcherrima* Skottsb.) has fruits over two centimeters (0.8 inch) in diameter. The fruits are

occasionally confused with the edible 'ōhelo (*Vaccinium* spp.), since they are similar in shape and color and the bush has a similar growth habit. However, 'ākia has a single seed per fruit while the edible 'ōhelo has many seeds. Also, the floral scar of 'ākia is a single dot but the scar on the 'ōhelo is a circle.

Toxicity of the 'ākia is variable and this variability is not fully understood. Friends of mine have eaten 'ākia without ill effects. Marie Neal (N, 616) says that the plant is nontoxic to mammals, but Dr. Frank Tabrah of the University of Hawaii Medical School has extracted from the whole plant some substances which are toxic to mice. It would be well to avoid eating these fruits. (Frank Tabrah, unpublished data)

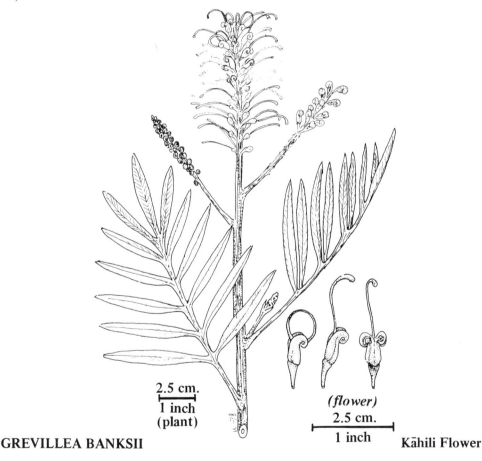

2.5 cm.
1 inch
(plant)

(flower)
2.5 cm.
1 inch

GREVILLEA BANKSII   Kāhili Flower

Grevillea banksii R. Br. (kāhili flower)

The plant is native to Australia. In Hawaii it is grown in gardens and parks as an ornamental, small tree. It is locally called "kāhili flower" because it resembles the feathered staffs used by the Hawaiians. (Another unrelated plant, *Lagerstroemia* spp., p. 41 is also called "kāhili flower.") The red or pale yellowish flowers grow on a spike, and they may be easily recognized by the style of the flower, which loops back into the flower until ready for pollination. The leaves are pinnately compound, pale green to grayish green.

According to Harry L. Arnold Jr. of Straub Clinic in Honolulu kāhili flower causes a dermatitis very similar to that from poison ivy (*Toxicodendron* spp.). As with poison ivy only some people are sensitive, but the two toxins seem to be completely unrelated to each other. A person sensitive to poison ivy may or may not be sensitive to kāhili flowers. Apparently the flower is the only part of the plant which causes symptoms. The chemical nature of the toxin is unknown. (Ar.)

For two or three days there usually are no symptoms, though some people may have symptoms after only a day. The skin reddens and blisters, with intense itching. The symptoms last for several days. (Ar.)

FIRST AID: There is very little one can do for this type of dermatitis. It is not dangerous but it is excruciating. See a physician for relief of symptoms.

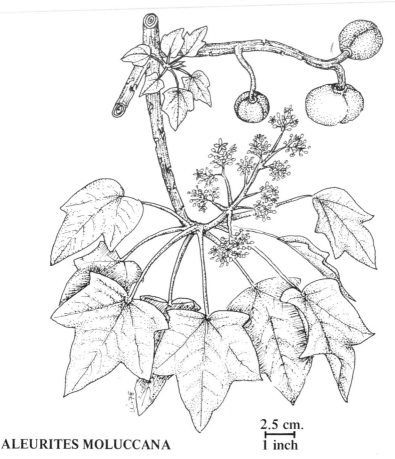

ALEURITES MOLUCCANA   2.5 cm.
                                       ├──────┤
                                       1 inch   Kukui

Aleurites moluccana (L.) Willd. (kukui, candlenut)

Kukui was probably brought into Hawaii from the south Pacific by the Polynesians but it has been here long enough to segregate into several varieties. The trees grow quite large, globular in shape, to heights as great as twenty meters (sixty feet). They grow wild in groves wherever surface water is plentiful. From a distance they can be spotted by their pale green foliage which stands out against the darker green of other trees. The leaves are palmately lobed and grow up to twenty centimeters (eight inches) long. The leaves of the typical kukui have three to five broad lobes, and some varieties have narrower, pointed lobes. The plant is monoecious, with male and female flowers together in panicles. The individual flowers are tiny and greenish yellow. The fruits are nuts about the size of black walnuts. The husk of the nuts is green, darkening to brown or black. It separates easily from the shells. The nut-shells are black or brown, covered with a white coating which rubs off with difficulty. The shell and nutmeat are quite oily. The shells can be polished simply by persistent rubbing with the fingers and they are frequently made into jewelry.

Kukui is a very useful tree to the Polynesians. The nuts are sparingly edible when cooked -- their extreme oiliness makes them laxative. The use of the nuts as jewelry has already been mentioned. In the past the nuts were used throughout Polynesia in torches and lamps (whence the name "candlenut".)

Kukui nuts contain a purgative oil and saponins. The oil is altered by cooking so raw kukui seeds are more strongly cathartic than cooked ones. Four seeds are sufficient to cause diarrhea. (K, 182; A, 26; Q, 491; H, 112) It is not dangerously poisonous, however, except to small children. The diarrhea disappears after a short time, and a physician needs to be consulted only if the symptoms persist or are severe.

Euphorbia spp.

Euphorbia is a large genus of plants from all over the world. There are some native Hawaiian species. Others come from Asia, Africa and both North and South America. They are extremely varied in appearance. Some species have broad leaves, both green and colored. For example, *E. pulcherrima* Willd. (poinsettia) has broad, green leaves and the blossoms are actually bright red leaves surrounding a cluster of tiny yellow flowers. Some varieties of poinsettia have white floral leaves. *E. tirucalli* L. (pencil plant) has succulent stems about the thickness of a pencil. It is thornless and leaves are so tiny that the stems appear leafless. Other *Euphorbias*, like *E. antiquorum* L. (Malayan spurge tree), look something like cacti, with thorns, succulent stems and often without leaves. *E. milii* des Moulin (crown of thorns) has both leaves and thorns on a woody stem.

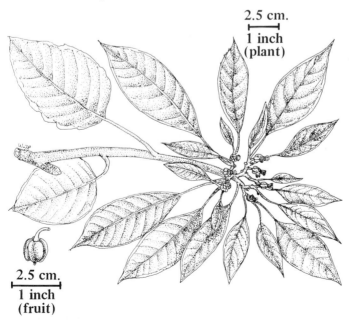

2.5 cm.
1 inch
(plant)

2.5 cm.
1 inch
(fruit)

EUPHORBIA PULCHERRIMA   Poinsetta

E. pulcherrima (poinsettia) deserves some special mention. This plant has been considered dangerously poisonous, but the statements all seem to relate to a single death in 1919, reported by Dr. Harry L. Arnold Sr. (A, 17). My own sister and brother, when they were small children, sucked on poinsetta leaves and soon afterward had diarrhea. Others have had similar reactions, but some cases have been reported where people ate poinsettia without ill effects. (Dr. Rea Chittenden, personal communication) There are probably variety differences -- some poinsettias may be more toxic than others -- and some people may be more susceptible than others to the toxins. This deserves further study and until this is done it would be prudent to avoid eating poinsettias and to induce vomiting in anyone who has eaten them. However, poinsettias are not dangerously toxic. As long as they are not eaten they are safe either as a yard ornamental or a house plant.

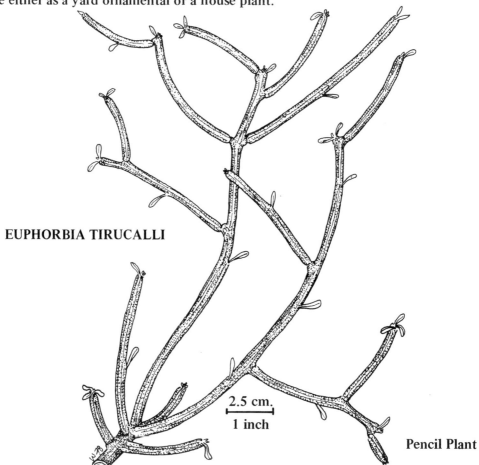

EUPHORBIA TIRUCALLI

2.5 cm.
1 inch

Pencil Plant

E. tirucalli (pencil plant), *E. milii* (crown of thorns) and *E. marginata* Pursh (snow on the mountain) cause skin irritation. Symptoms include intense itching and burning where the milky sap has come into contact with the skin. Taken internally most species of Euphorbia cause vomiting and diarrhea. (A, 17; H, 112; K, 185; Q, 502)

FIRST AID: *External*: If skin symptoms appear while you are handling the plants wash the affected areas with clear (preferably cold) water for at least five

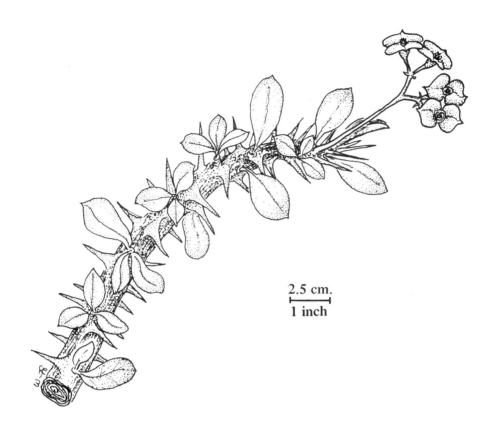

2.5 cm.
1 inch

EUPHORBIA MILII   Crown of Thorns

minutes. No further treatment is likely to be needed. If the sap gets into the eyes, wash the eyes with cold, clear water for at least five minutes and take the patient to a physician.

Internal: Induce vomiting if it has not already occurred. Do not attempt to check spontaneous vomiting and diarrhea. Take the patient to a physician if the symptoms persist or are severe.

Pedilanthus tithimaloides Poit. (slipper flower, redbird cactus)

The slipper flower is native to the West Indies. In Hawaii it is grown in gardens, particularly in rock gardens. It is a low, sprawling shrub with succulent, usually zigzag stems. The sap is milky. At each stem joint is an ovate, shiny leaf five to ten centimeters (two to four inches) long. The leaves fall soon after forming, so frequently the stem is bare except near the growing tip. The blossom is actually a monoecious inflorescence with a female flower and several male flowers. These are surrounded by two bright red bracts about one centimeter (0.4 inch) long, which some people liken in shape to a slipper or bird (whence the common names).

Slipper flower is in the same family as *Euphorbia* (see above) and it is symptomatically very similar. The sap is irritating to the skin and gastrointestional tract. It causes reddening of the skin with intense itching and burning within a few minutes

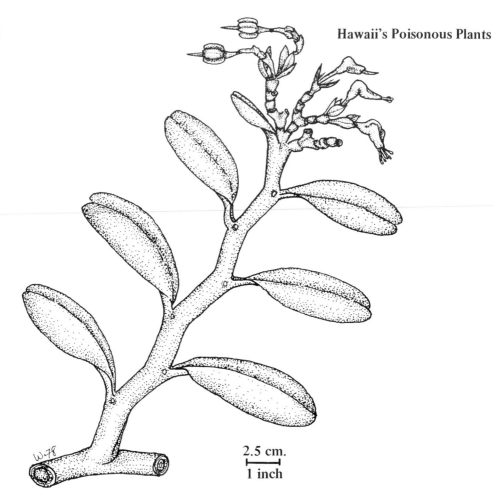

2.5 cm.
1 inch

PEDILANTHUS TITHIMALOIDES   Slipper Flower

after contact. Taken internally it quickly causes vomiting and diarrhea. (Q, 525)
     FIRST AID: If the sap gets on the skin wash the affected area with clear water
for at least five minutes. If it gets into the eyes wash the eyes with clear water for
five minutes and consult a physician. If taken internally induce vomiting if it hasn't
already occurred and take the patient to a physician.

Melia azedarach L. (chinaberry, pride of India)
     The chinaberry comes from the Himalaya mountains. It is grown in Hawaii as
an ornamental tree in yards and parks. It becomes a large tree, to twenty meters (sixty feet) high, but it is often also kept trimmed to a small bush. The leaves are bipin-
nately compound, fifteen to fifty centimeters (seven to twenty inches) long, often
clustered near the tips of the branches. The flowers are bright lavender, in panicles
which bloom in the spring. The fruit is a golden-yellow spherical drupe about one
centimeter (0.4 inch) in diameter.
     Chinaberry has two toxins, a resin (azadarin) and an alkaloid (paraisine). It is
very poisonous, six to eight seeds having killed a child. All parts of the plants are
toxic, but poisonings have occured mainly when children ate the fruits or made
"tea" of the leaves. (H, 100; K, 206; Q, 482)

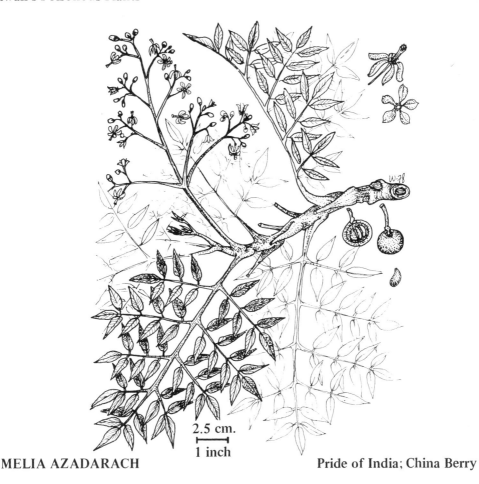

2.5 cm.
1 inch

MELIA AZADARACH   Pride of India; China Berry

Chinaberry causes vomiting, diarrhea or constipation, weak pulse, difficulty in breathing and paralysis. (H, 100; K, 206)

FIRST AID: Induce vomiting if it has not already occurred. Do not attempt to check spontaneous vomiting and diarrhea. If the patient has stopped breathing administer artificial respiration. Take the patient to a physician.

Erythroxylum coca Lam. (coca, cocaine plant)

Coca is used by people in its native South America for its stimulant effects. It is illegal to grow in the United States (See *Papaver,* p. 35) so one is not likely to find it in Hawaii. It is a shrub, one to four meters (three to twelve feet) high. The leaves are oval with blunt tips. Each leaf has two or four longitudinal lines and several veins along the midrib. The leaves are three to eight centimeters (one to three inches) long. The flowers, about one centimeter (0.4 inch) across, are clustered at the leaf axils. The fruit is a red drupe.

The main toxin in coca leaves is the tropane alkaloid, cocaine. Poisoning is not likely from the plant, but more likely from deliberate ingestion of the drug, illegally obtained. Cocaine is a powerful stimulant of the central nervous system. Initial symptoms are restlessness, hallucinations, rapid heartbeat, dilated pupils and muscular spasms. Later symptoms include irregular respiration, convulsions and coma. (Cr,

272; Dr, 271; Q, 443) However, the main danger from cocaine is its addicting properties. A chronic taker of cocaine is likely to become a paranoid psychotic with bizarre hallucinations of insects and imaginary creatures crawling over his skin. (CR, 272ff)

FIRST AID: Wash the skin and mouth with clear water to remove any unabsorbed drug. To retard absorption of ingested cocaine, give the patient water, milk or activated charcoal and induce vomiting. Take the patient to a physician. (Dr, 272)

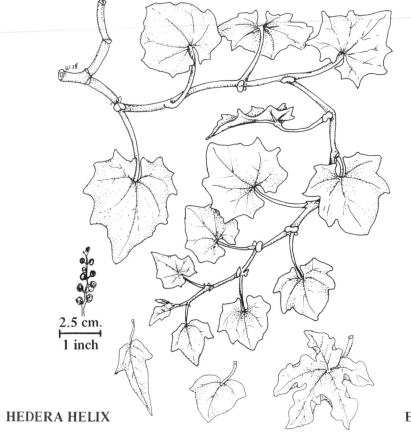

2.5 cm.
1 inch

HEDERA HELIX   English Ivy

Hedera helix L. (English Ivy)

English ivy is a native to Europe and Asia. It is becoming common in Hawaii, where it is grown in yards and gardens, especially in cooler areas. It grows as an evergreen, woody, climbing vine on other plants or on the sides of stone walls and buildings. The leaves are alternate, three-lobed, about five centimeters (two inches) long. The shape of the leaf varies, there being many horticultural varieties, but the commonest is the typical ivy with broad, pointed lobes. The flowers are inconspicuous and greenish. The fruits are three- to five-seeded berries in clusters of up to ten berries.

The toxin is an irritant saponic glycoside, hederagenin, found in the leaves and fruit. Symptoms include diarrhea, excitement and difficulty in breathing. (K, 371; H, 106) Poisonings have never been reported in Hawaii, and they are not very likely here, because the most attractive and most toxic part, the fruit, rarely forms here. Children in the mainland have been poisoned by eating the fruits or drinking "tea" made from the leaves. (H, 106)

FIRST AID: Induce vomiting and take the patient to a physician. Administer artificial respiration if the patient is not breathing.

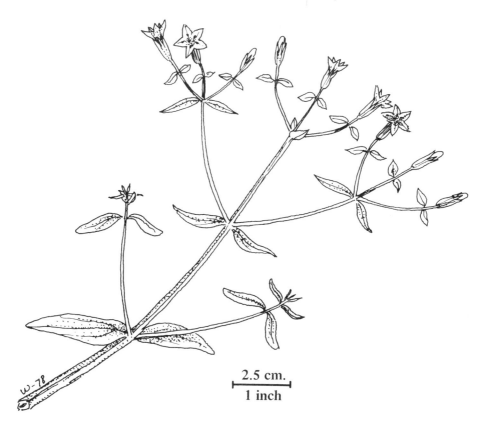

2.5 cm.
1 inch

CENTAURIUM UMBELLATUM   Mountain Pink

Centaurium umbellatum Gilib. (mountain pink, centaury)

This plant is native to Europe. In Hawaii it grows as a small herbaceous pasture weed to a height of forty centimeters (sixteen inches). There are two types of leaves: four to six centimeter (1.5 to 2.5 inches) basal leaves in rosettes, and smaller, oppositely arranged leaves along the stems. The attractive, pink flowers are about one centimeter (0.4 inch) long. They grow in clusters near the stem tips. The fruit is a two-valved capsule.

The toxins of *Centaurium* are unknown, but they are extremely irritating to the gastrointestional tract. My mother became nauseated after only tasting the plant accidently. Larger doses cause vomiting and diarrhea. (K, 260)

FIRST AID: Induce vomiting if it has not occurred already. Do not attempt to check spontaneous vomiting or diarrhea. See a physician if the symptoms persist or are severe.

ALLAMANDA CATHARTICA

2.5 cm.
1 inch

Allamanda

Allamanda cathartica L. (allamanda, nani-ali'i, lani-ali'i)

Allamanda is native to Brazil. It is grown in gardens, yards and parks as an ornamental in Hawaii and throughout the tropics. It grows on all islands at low elevations, near human habitation. The plant is a woody vine which can be trained and pruned to become a handsome hedge. Allowed to grow and twine into trees it can attain any height that the tree does. I have seen allamandas growing in large mango trees, making the mango tree appear to be bearing allamanda flowers. The leaves are shiny, bright green, lanceolate, ten to fifteen centimeters (four to six inches) long, and arranged in pairs, threes and fours along the stem. The flowers are bright yellow. The variety most common in Hawaii has flowers about ten centimeters (four inches) across. The flowers have a cup-shaped center and broad petal lobes.

In times past allamanda was used medicinally as a cathartic. The poison is in the milky sap. In moderate amounts it causes diarrhea, and in larger amounts it causes both vomiting and diarrhea. (K, 262; Q, 719)

FIRST AID: Induce vomiting if it has not already occurred. See a physician if the symptoms persist or are severe.

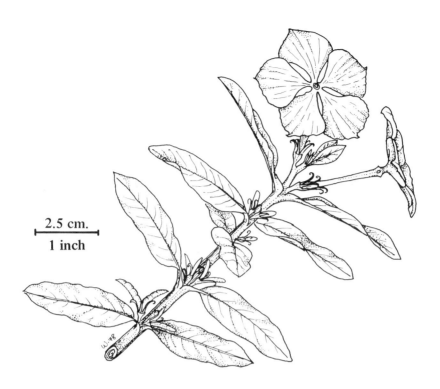

2.5 cm.
1 inch

CATHARANTHUS ROSEUS   Kīhāpai; Periwinkle

Catharanthus roseus (L.) G. Don (periwinkle, kīhāpai).

Periwinkles are very popular in yards, gardens, parks and schoolgrounds in Hawaii. They grow as small shrub thirty to sixty centimeters (one to two feet) high. The leaves are paired along the stem. Each leaf is two to eight centimeters (one to three inches) long, ovate-lanceolate with a point at the tip. It has pink, white or purple flowers with sometimes a red center. Each flower has a two-centimeter (one inch) long tube terminating in five broad petal lobes. The lobes do not overlap but are broad enough nearly to touch along the lateral edges. The flower is about three centimeters (1.3 inches) in diameter.

Periwinkles contain the indole alkaloids, vincristine and vinblastine, used in cancer therapy. Acute toxicity is low but these drugs are teratogenic (i.e., they cause deformities of the unborn when the pregnant mother eats the plant.) Human poisonings are rare but stock poisonings are commoner. (ACS, 473; Q, 725)

Cerbera manghas L. (cerbera, reva) and *C. tanghin* Hook. (ordeal bean)

Cerbera is from Polynesia and southwestern Asia. In Hawaii it is grown in yards as an ornamental. It is not very common, but common enough to be a potential cause of poisoning. It grows as a handsome, rounded tree with crooked branches to a height of three meters (nine feet). The leaves are glossy green, fifteen to thirty centimeters (six to twelve inches) long. It has cymes of white flowers, somewhat smaller than plumeria (below) but similar, with pink or yellow centers. The fruits are large

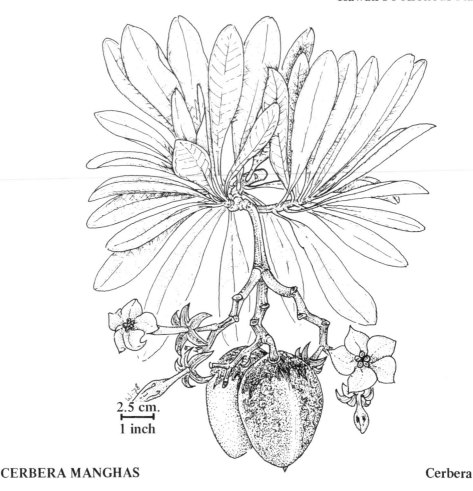

2.5 cm.
1 inch

CERBERA MANGHAS   Cerbera

drupes, green to purplish and shaped like a mango. Because of this shape they may tempt a person to try to eat them, but they are extremely bitter to the taste.

According to Quisumbing and to Neal, cerbera has two different kinds of toxins. One, in the latex (milky sap) of any part of the plant, is highly irritant, causing blindness if it gets into the eyes and diarrhea and vomiting if taken internally. The other toxin is the cardiac glycoside, cerberin, which is similar to digitalin (see *Digitalis,* p. 62). The pure cerberin has a symptom-producing dose of about 0.6 mg. for an adult human. (A, 32; Q, 727; N, 692)

FIRST AID: If the latex gets into the eyes wash with clear water for at least five minutes. If either latex or the seed is taken internally induce vomiting immediately and take the patient to a physician without delay. Speed is essential.

Plumeria spp. (plumeria, frangipani)

Plumeria is native to the West Indies. As elsewhere in the tropics it is an extremely popular tree in Hawaii with its white, yellow, pink or dark, purplish-red flowers. There are also hybrids with intermediate colors, including a beautiful salmon-pink variety. The flowers have a narrow tube terminating in five broad, rounded petal lobes. The leaves are lanceolate, up to thirty centimeters (one foot) long. The tree has thickened, succulent stems which are only somewhat woody. When bro-

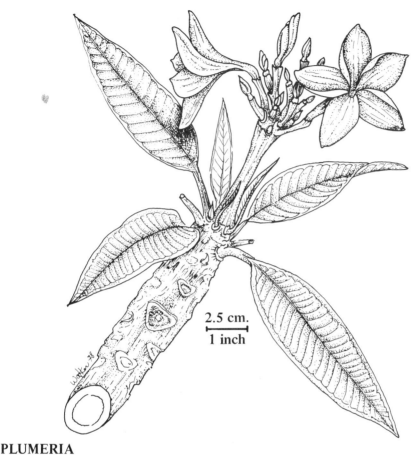

2.5 cm.
1 inch

PLUMERIA   Plumeria

ken any part of the plant exudes a copious milky sap. Occasionally the tree grows as high as eight meters (twenty-five feet) but more commonly it is not over three meters (nine feet) high.

Plumeria has a cathartic substance, plumerid, in all parts of the plant. It is not very toxic and it is included in this book only because there have been some cases where people have been poisoned by eating plumeria salads. (Q, 732; R. Chittenden, personal communication) Diarrhea occurs about five fours after a person eats plumerias.

FIRST AID: If a person has eaten plumeria flowers and has not yet shown symptoms, induce vomiting. The diarrhea will run its course in a few hours. Consult a physician only if symptoms persist or are severe.

Calotropis gigantea (L.) R. Br. (crownflower, pua-kalaunu)

Crownflower, a native of southern Asia and Indonesia, is a shrub up to five meters (fifteen feet) high. The pale leaves are oval, 8 to 25 centimeters (three to ten inches) long, hairy on the underside. The flowers are lavender or white, about four centimeters (1.5 inches) across, with curled-back petals and a five-sided, prominent corona (the "crown"). It seldom fruits in Hawaii.

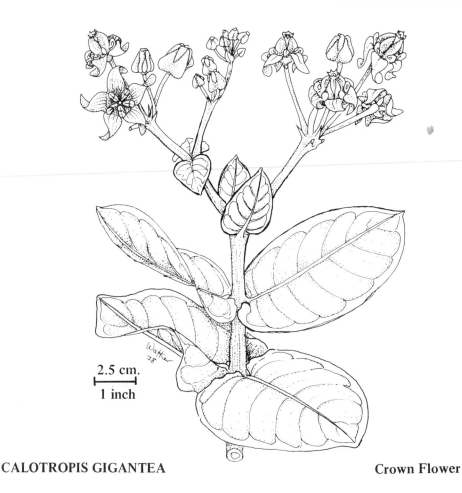

2.5 cm.

1 inch

CALOTROPIS GIGANTEA   **Crown Flower**

Another species, *C. procera* (Jacq.) R. Br. is rare in Hawaii. It is smaller than *C. gigantea* and its flowers are smaller and the petals are erect, rather than curled.

Crownflowers are strung into leis, but these should be worn with caution, since many people contact skin irritation from these plants. Others, however, may handle and wear them without irritation.

All parts of the plant are poisonous. If the milky sap gets into the eyes it causes conjunctivitis, and sometimes blindness. Eating or chewing any part will cause vomiting and diarrhea. The toxin is an irritant resin, calotropin. (H, 133; A, 31; Q, 744)

FIRST AID: If irritation occurs externally or if the sap gets into the eyes wash the affected area with clear water for at least five minutes. If taken internally induce vomiting if it has not already occurred. Do not attempt to check spontaneous vomiting or diarrhea. Take the patient to a physician.

Cestrum nocturnum L. (night blooming cestrum, fragrance of the night, 'ala-aumoe, kūpaoa)

Night blooming cestrum is from the West Indies. It grows well in the lowlands of Hawaii in yards, gardens and parks. It is a shrub with long stems, panicles of tiny, greenish-white flowers that open at night, and white, fleshy berries. It sends out a fragrance during the evening which can be detected a block away. The fragrance is

Fragrance of the Night

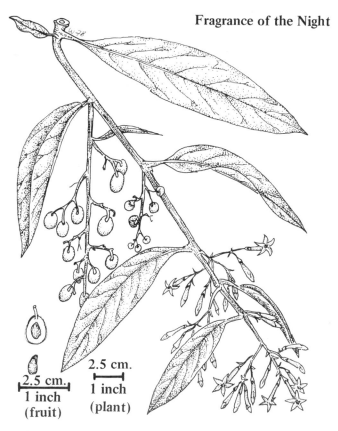

2.5 cm.
1 inch
(fruit)

2.5 cm.
1 inch
(plant)

CESTRUM NOCTURNUM   Night Blooming Cestrum;

delightful, but if the flowers are brought into the house the odor may be too strong to be pleasant.

Day blooming cestrum, *C. diurnum* L. is also from the West Indies. It has white flowers and black berries and it is fragrant by day. Another species, *C. aurantiacum* Lindl. (orange cestrum) is somewhat viny and it has orange flowers.

All of the cestrums contain tropane alkaloids similar to atropine. They are not as toxic as *Datura* (p. 27) but they are still highly poisonous. It is interesting that the cestrums contain the same alkaloids as *Datura* but the symptoms are somewhat different; for example, *Datura* reduces salivation (the mouth feels dry) while *Cestrum* increases it. (K, 278; H, 136)

Cestrum causes hallucinations, rapid heartbeat, elevated temperatures, irritability, difficulty in breathing and paralysis. The patient salivates excessively and becomes dizzy and nauseated. (k, 278; H, 136)

FIRST AID: Induce vomiting and take the patient to a physician. Administer artificial respiration if the patient has stopped breathing.

Nicotiana spp. (tobacco)
Several species of tobacco grow in Hawaii and all are native to America. The tobacco of commerce *(N. tabacum* L.) is a large herb, two meters (six feet) high. The

leaves are oblong, about thirty centimeters (one foot) long. Although the plant grows well in Hawaii, poisoning is more likely from children eating cigarettes than from the fresh plants. Fortunately nicotine from tobacco is poorly absorbed and proves less toxic than the content of the alkaloid would indicate. At the same time, the nicotine can be absorbed through the skin. People have been poisoned when trying to smuggle tobacco leaves against their skin and inside their clothing. Nicotine is a pyridine alkaloid. Symptoms include severe vomiting, diarrhea, abdominal pain, shivering, elevated temperature (but with cold extremities). The pulse is at first voilent, then rapid and weak. There may be difficulty in breathing. Symptoms appear rapidly after ingestion. (K, 286; H, 141; PT, 522)

FIRST AID: Induce vomiting and take the patient to a physician. Speed is esestial, since nicotine is a rapid acting poison.

2.5 cm.

1 inch

SOLANDRA HARTWEGII   Cup of Gold

Solandra grandiflora Sw. (silvercup) and *S. hartwegii* N.E. Br. (cup of gold)

The silvercup comes from the West Indies and the cup of gold from Mexico. They are grown in Hawaii in yards, parks and hotel grounds. They are woody shrubs or vines growing high into trees. The smooth leaves are oblong, five to fifteen centimeters (two to six inches) long. The most spectacular part of these plants is the 25 centimeter (ten inch) long, cup-shaped flowers with five petal lobes. The cup of gold is yellow and the silvercup is white. The flowers are fragrant but not altogether pleasant.

Both species of Solandra are toxic, containing the steroid-glycosidal alkaloid, solanine. For symptoms and first aid see *Solanum* (p. 73) (H, 141; K, 287)

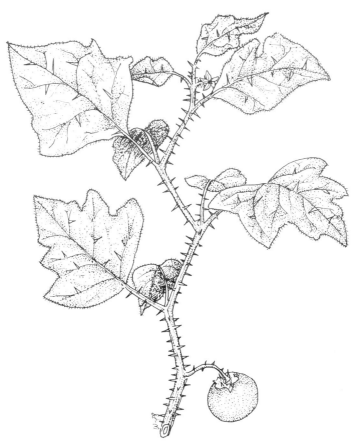

SOLANUM ACULEATISSIMUM   Kīkānia Lei

Solanum spp. (A, 53; H, 141; K, 287; Q, 141)
This genus is covered also on p. 73. The inedible species are these:
S. aculeatissimum Jacq. (kīkānia-lei, akaaka, red pōpolo) is from tropical A-merica. It grows as a weedy shrub up to one meter (three feet) high. The leaves, stems and buds are covered with yellow thorns. The leaves are pinnately lobed, seven to twenty centimeters (three to eight inches) long. The fruits are red spheres with dry pulp and many seeds, two to three centimeters (about one inch) in diameter. All parts of the plant are poisonous to eat.
S. sodomeum L. (apple of Sodom, pōpolo kīkānia) is native to the Mediterra-nean. It grows as an extremely thorny shrub to 1.5 meters (four feet) high in pas-tures and fields of the drier parts of Hawaii. It is similar in appearance to *S. aculea-tissimum*. The fruits are about five centimeters (two inches) in diameter and bright golden yellow. The flowers are purple and resemble those of potatoes. The fruits of both apple of Sodom and kīkānia-lei are strung into leis, and as such are safe to use. All parts of the plant are poisonous to eat.

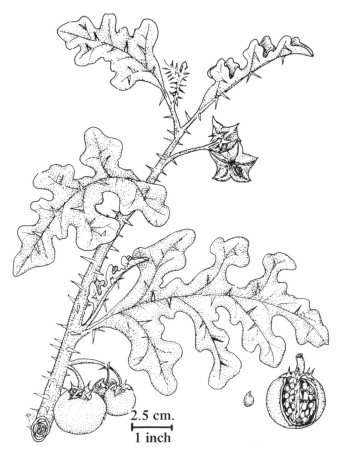

2.5 cm.
1 inch

SOLANUM SODOMEUM   Apple of Sodom

   S. pseudocapsicum L. (Jerusalem cherry) is from Europe and Asia. It grows wild along roadsides and in open forests of Hawaii. It is also grown as an ornamental shrub in yards and gardens. It grows up to 1.5 meter (four inches) high. The leaves are lanceolate, about five centimeters (two inches) long. It has bright orange berries about one centimeter (0.4 inch) across. The flowers look much like tomato flowers, white in color. Some authorities consider the berries poisonous while others say they are harmless. (N, 744) Typical *Solanum* alkaloids have been isolated from all parts of the plant, so it is potentially toxic and the berries should not be eaten. (K, 292)
   Symptoms and toxicity of *Solanum* are discussed on p. 73.
   FIRST AID: Induce vomiting if it has not already occurred. Do not attempt to check spontaneous vomiting and diarrhea. Consult a physician.

Lantana camara L. (lantana)
   Lantana originated in tropical and subtropical America and it was brought to Hawaii as an ornamental. It escaped and now covers lowland areas throughout the islands. It is especially common by the seashore, for it is quite tolerant of sea spray. It grows as a bush with tiny, sharp thorns on the stems. The rough, ovate leaves are very aromatic and they may be smelled some distance from the plant on warm days.

2.5 cm.
1 inch

SOLANUM PSEUDOCAPSICUM   Jerusalem Cherry

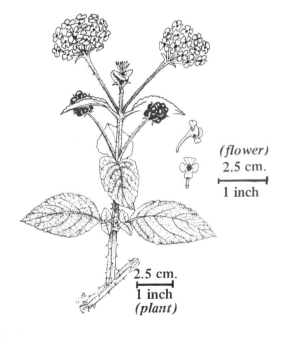

(flower)
2.5 cm.
1 inch

2.5 cm.
1 inch
(plant)

LANTANA CAMARA   Lantana

The bushes are generally one meter (three feet) high but they may grow taller than a man. The flowers grow in small heads, the wild ones with the outer, older flowers pink and the central, younger ones orange. The berries are tiny and blue-black in color. Cultivated varieties have flowers of many colors, from yellow through orange and red to pink and lavender. There are thornless varieties.

The toxin of lantana is the polycyclic triterpenoid, lantadene A. It is a hepatogenic photosensitizer (i.e., it damages the liver, which in turn makes substances which cause the person to become highly sensitive to sunlight. See p. 86). Actually lantana is only moderately toxic, but it is dangerous because it has berries so delicious that a person eating any at all will likely eat toxic quantities. The unfortunate thing about lantana is that the liver damage is largely irreversible. (K, 296; H, 135; K, 55)

The symptoms of lantana poisoning include severe vomiting and diarrhea, muscular weakness and circulatory collapse. Because of the higher sensitivity to sunlight the person is also likely to have symptoms of sunburn and sunstroke; reddening, burning and itching of the skin; dazzling of the eyes; strong, rapid heartbeat, elevated temperature and general weakness.

FIRST AID: Induce vomiting and take the patient to a physician. If the temperature seems elevated apply cold compresses to the face and forearms. The patient should avoid exposure to the sun for some time afterwards. The physician can advise him when it is safe to go into the sun again.

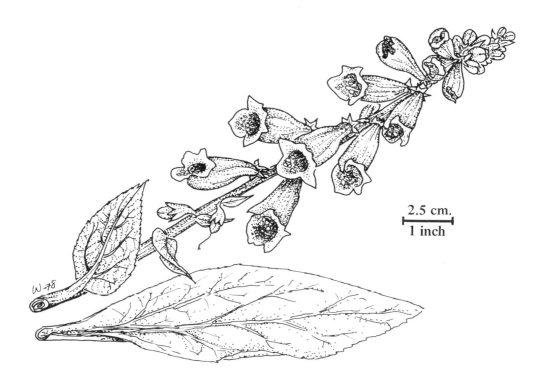

2.5 cm.
1 inch

DIGITALIS PURPUREA   Foxglove

Digitalis purpurea L. (foxglove)

Foxgloves are native to western Europe. They have long been a favorite garden flower in the temperate regions of the world. Foxgloves grow well in Hawaii only at higher elevations. They grow as a 1.5 meter (four foot) high, herbaceous, short-lived perennial. The leaves are ovate to lanceolate in shape, alternately arranged along the usually unbranched stem. The basal leaves are about thirty centimeters (one foot) long, becoming progessively shorter up the stem. The flowers are bell-shaped, pendulous, about eight centimeters (three inches) long in terminal racemes. They are purple, red, white or pink and usually spotted.

The toxins of *Digitalis* are cardiac glycosides. The most important and best-known of these is digitalin (also called digitoxin or digitalis), an extremely useful heart stimulant drug. Digitalin causes an increase in the force of systolic contractions and increases the duration of diastole. The result is a slower, stronger heartbeat. This effect occurs only in carefully controlled clinical doses, however. (Dr, 332; K, 301, PT, 18)

Harry L. Arnold, Jr., (personal communication) informs me that foxgloves grown in Hawaii have been analyzed and found to be free of any toxin.

Overdoses of digitalin, either from eating the plant or from too much of the drug, cause vomiting, diarrhea (followed by constipation) and abdominal pain. Vision may blur and the patient becomes drowsy. The heartbeat at first becomes stronger and slower, then irregular. Death occurs from cardiac failure, the heart stopping in systolic contraction (i.e., "in systole"). (K, 301; PT, 18)

FIRST AID: Induce vomiting if it has not already occurred. Keep the patient quiet and take him to a physician. Speed is essential, since the cardiac glycosides are rapid-acting poisons.

Eupatorium adenophorum Spreng. (pā-makani haole, snakeroot)

The plant is native to Mexico. It was first introduced onto Maui and has since spread to all of the major Hawaiian islands. It is a common roadside weed, growing occasionally to nearly two meters (six feet) but more commonly about thirty centimeters (one foot) high. It looks much like *Ageratum*, a hairy aromatic herb with o-vate, pointed leaves five to fifteen centimeters (two to six inches) long. The leaf margins are crenate. The blossom is a cluster of white pompom-shaped heads, each head five millimeters (1/5 inch) across. The clusters are somewhat sparser than those of *Ageratum*.

The active toxin is the complex alcohol, tremetol. It was the cause of a puzzling ailment ("milk sickness") in the eastern United States during the 1800's. At one time it was a major cause of death in the United States. It wasn't until 1927 that the cause of the disease was traced to *E. rugosum* Houtt., a close relative. It has not caused death by humans eating the plant, but when cows have eaten the plant in quantity the toxin accumulates in the milk, which is then toxic to humans. The cow may have toxic milk without herself showing symptoms. This disease is not likely to be a problem with commercial milk, but milk from a family farm may easily be toxic. Actually no cases of milksickness have occurred in Hawaii and this plant is included in this book mainly to alert people to eradicate it in pastures. (K, 397)

Araceae

This is a large family of mostly herbaceous plants from all over the tropical parts of the world. Leaves are quite varied, with some heart-shaped, others deeply cleft and still others lanceolate. Venation may be parallel or netted. The most characteristic trait of this family is the fleshy spike of tiny flowers subtended by a large, usually colorful or white bract (green forms exist also). Most of the plants in this fa-

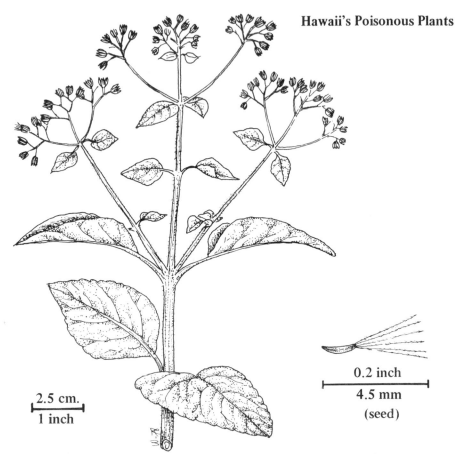

0.2 inch
4.5 mm
(seed)

2.5 cm.
1 inch

EUPATORIUM ADENOPHORUM   Snakeroot

mily contain calcium oxalate crystals (raphides), which cause irritation, stinging and pain in the mouth and throat when the plant is chewed. Toxicity varies from species to species, and even within a species, from nontoxic to highly toxic. *Anthurium* spp. contain so little toxin that symptoms are practically nonexistent. Taro (*Colocasia esculenta*, p. 74) is toxic when raw but edible when cooked. *Dieffenbachia* spp. (p. 30) are dangerously toxic, but their toxicity is partly due to other substances. In general avoid eating or chewing any plant in this family unless you know it is safe. Here are some plants in this family most often mentioned as toxic: (K, 472; Q, 137ff)

Acorus calamus L. (sweet flag) from eastern Asia.
Aglaonema spp. from eastern Asia, Indonesia and the Philippines.
        (This plant may easily be confused with *Dieffenbachia*, p. 30)
Alocasia spp. from southeastern Asia and tropical America.
Amorphophallus spp. from tropical Asia, Borneo and the Philippines
Caladium spp. (caladium) from South America
Colocasia spp. See below and on p.
Dieffenbachia spp. (dumbcane) from tropical America. See p. 30.
Philodendron spp. from tropical America.
Pistia stratiotes L. (water lettuce) from Asia and Africa.
Zantedeschia spp. (calla lilies) from Africa.

Alocasia spp.; *Caladium* spp.; *Colocasia* spp. (See also p. 74).

These genera originated in southern Asia. They grow well in Hawaii and are frequently found in yards and gardens. Occasionally they are found escaped in fields. They are so similar that they are frequently confused with each other. Since they include both edible and toxic plants they are frequent causes of poisoning, though luckily even the most toxic of these plants are not dangerously so (though they may make a person quite uncomfortable for a while). All of these plants have heart-shaped leaves and fleshy corms. The leaves are net-veined. The plants are stemless except for the corms. Some varieties of *Caladium* are variegated green, pink and white.

There is no sure way to distinguish the edible from the toxic species short of knowing the characteristics of each species and variety. In general the variegated species are all toxic, but many all-green plants are also poisonous. The best way for the home gardener raising vegetables to be sure is to obtain cuttings which are known to be edible and grow them. One should remember that all of these plants are toxic when raw. If in doubt nibble a piece of the cooked plants before eating any. If it does not cause burning or prickling in the mouth within a short while it is safe to eat.

FIRST AID: Rinse out the mouth with clear water. If often helps to suck ice cubes to relieve the pain. No further treatment is necessary, except for the patient's comfort, unless toxic pieces of the plant are swallowed. If any plant material is swallowed induce vomiting immediately.

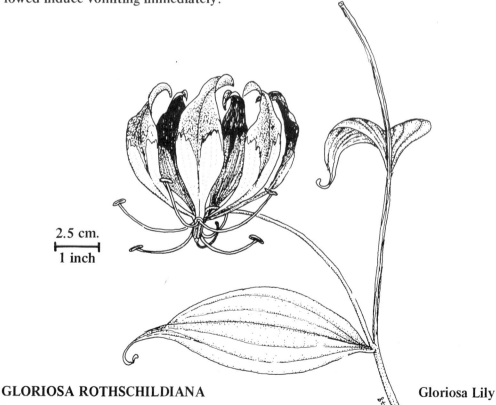

2.5 cm.
1 inch

GLORIOSA ROTHSCHILDIANA   Gloriosa Lily

Gloriosa rothschildiana O'Brien and *G. superba* L. (gloriosa lily)

Gloriosa lilies originated in Africa and they are now grown as a garden flower throughout Hawaii. The bright red and yellow flowers grown in a vine, thirty to sixty centimeters (one to two feet) high. The alternately arranged, lanceolate leaves end in tendrils which clasp nearby plants. When they first bloom the flowers are mostly yellow with a narrow, red stripe down the middle of the petal. The red stripe widens as the flower ages, until the petals of older flowers are almost entirely red. The flowers bend downward, but the petals are reflexed, so they appear to point upwards.*G. rothschildiana* has petals somewhat wider and less curled along the edges than *G. superba*. All-yellow varieties exist also and development of horticultural varieties has blurred the difference between the two species.

The poisons of gloriosa lilies are colchicine and a related substance, superbine. I have no numerical data about the toxicity of the plant but all of the sources list gloriosa as "highly toxic." Colchicine and superbine are similar to alkaloids, but since they are acidic rather than alkaline in reaction they are not true alkaloids. Colchicine is used in genetic experiments because it stops cell division without preventing chromosome duplication. Thus geneticists are able to use colchicine to obtain plants with extra numbers of chromosomes. It could probably cause similar aberrations in humans, but this is not its primary action as a toxin. Colchicine and superbine are irritants and nerve poisons. (A, 39; H, 44; K, 452; Q, 166; Dr, 266)

Gloriosa lilies cause immediate numbness and burning of the lips, tongue and throat. It is followed by vomiting, bleeding diarrhea, difficulty in breathing and convulsions. (K, 452; Dr, 266)

FIRST AID: Induce vomiting and take the patient to a physician. Apply artificial respiration if the patient has stopped breathing. Speed is essential.

CHAPTER IV
POISONOUS FOOD PLANTS

A number of the plants we use as sources of food are poisonous. These can be segregated into two groups: those plants from which the food obtained is toxic, and those from which the food is not toxic but the plant has other toxic parts. (We shall not concern ourselves with food plants which become toxic by disease or contamination.)

PLANTS YIELDING TOXIC FOOD SUBSTANCES

Myristica fragrans Houtt. (nutmeg) is the familiar spice. It is native to the Moluccas. The tree is extremely rare in Hawaii, but the spice is found in nearly every home. In the quantities used as a spice it is perfectly harmless. It has such a strong flavor that people are not likely to eat toxic quantities. However, it is sufficiently toxic that one seed (about ten grams or one tablespoon) can cause symptoms: euphoria and lightheadedness. Larger doses are not so pleasant: rapid heartbeat, excessive thirst, agitation, anxiety, stomach pain, delirium and difficulty with vision. (H, 51)

Beta vulgaris L. (beet, chard)
Both beets and chard are wholesome foods in normal quantities. Beet roots are not toxic but the leaves of both beets and chard contain varying amounts of soluble oxalates, which can upset the calcium balance in the blood and cause kidney damage. (K, 35) They will cause trouble only when eaten in large amounts over a long time. (perhaps as a main item in the meals)

Spinacia oleracea L. (spinach)
This has been much overrated as a source of iron. Like beet greens it contains soluble oxalates, sometimes in excess of ten per cent of the total dry weight. (K, 35) The oxalates render the iron unavailable for human nutrition, and the oxalates are likely to upset the calcium balance in the blood.

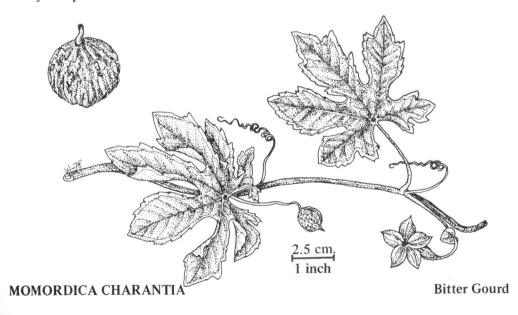

2.5 cm.
1 inch

MOMORDICA CHARANTIA   Bitter Gourd

Momordica charantia L. (bitter gourd, balsam apple, balsam pear)
This is a creeping vine with palmately lobed leaves fifteen centimeters (six inches) or less across. It has yellow trumpet-shaped flowers two to three centimeters (about one inch) across. The cultivated varieties have elongate, warty fruits as long as thirty centimeters (one foot). So far as I can determine the cultivated varieties are completely nontoxic. They are frequently sold in grocery stores to be used as a cooked vegetable. The wild varieties are toxic, the tough outer skin and the seeds both containing purgative substances. The reddish pulp around the seeds is edible. (K, 389; H, 112; Q, 944) The fruits of the wild varieties are ovoid, three to twelve centimeters (1.5 to 5 inches) across.

Amoracia rusticana (Lam.) Gaertn. (horseradish) is not often grown in Hawaii but foods flavored with it are frequently sold in stores. It contains the same substance as *Brassica* (below) and the same comments apply to it.

Brassica spp.: *B. caulorapa* Pasq. (kohlrabi); *B. chinensis* L. (chinese cabbage); *B. hirta* Moench (white mustard); *B. juncea* (L.) Czernj. & Coss (kai choi, leaf mustard); *B. napobrassica* Mill. (rutabaga); *B. nigra* (L.) Koch (black mustard); *B. oleracea* L. (cabbage, Brussels sprouts, kale, broccoli, cauliflower); *B. pekinensis* (Lour.) Rupr. (Chinese cabbage); *B. rapa* L. (turnip).
These are all well-known, useful garden vegetables and condiments. In the quantities normally used they are harmless and wholesome, though somewhat hard for some people to digest. They all contain sulfur compounds which give them their sharp and characteristic flavors and which are also responsible for their toxic properties. One group of these sulfur compounds can cause goiter if eaten in large quantities over a long time. Another group (the isothiocyanates or "mustard oils") are highly irritant. They cause the food to taste "hot." Put on the skin they feel warm and cause reddening, and this property is utilized in the counter-irritant liniments and mustard plasters. When eaten in sufficient amounts they cause vomiting and diarrhea. (K, 26; K, 28; K, 158ff; ACS, 483)

Raphanus sativus L. (radish, daikon) has the same toxins as Brassica (above) and the same comments apply to it.

Dolichos lablab L. (lablab bean, hyacinth bean)
Lablab beans are native to India. The plant grows as a climbing vine up to fifteen feet high. There are three leaflets to each leaf, similar to lima bean leaves but broader. The flowers are white or pink. The beans are distinctive, being dark red or brown with a white stripe along the edge. They contain a cyanogenic glycoside, which releases hydrocyanic acid. (H, 84; Q, 398) The glycoside can be removed by prolonged boiling and simmering and then throwing out the water. Lablab beans are used much like kidney beans in cooking and they are an important ingredient in Filipino cooking. When properly prepared they are safe to eat and an excellent source of protein.

Symptoms are those of cyanide poisoning. (See Manihot, p. 70)
FIRST AID: Induce vomiting if it has not already occurred. Administer oxygen if it is available. Take the patient to a physician immediately. Speed is essential, for cyanide is a rapid-acting poison.

Phaseolus limensis Macf. and *P. lunatus* L. (lima bean)
The white or light green, flattened lima beans common in the United States

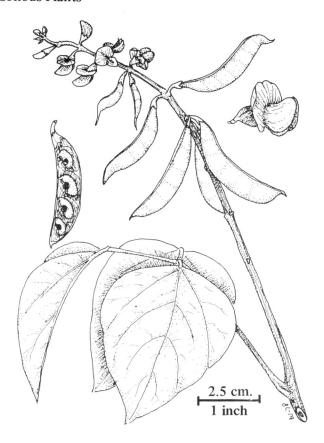

2.5 cm.
1 inch

DOLICHOS LABLAB   Lablab Bean

have been bred to be free of any toxin, but should you happen to find the darker or plumper varieties they can contain the cyanogenic glycoside, linamarin. Like lablab beans (above) these can be rendered safe by cooking them for a long time and throwing out the water. (K, 346; Q, 419; ACS, 519) for first aid see *Manihot* (below).

Vicia faba L. (fava bean, broadbean)
    Fava beans are a popular food among people in the Mediterranean countries. To most people fava beans are harmless and nutritious, but to people who are genetically deficient in the enzyme, glucose-6-phosphate dehydrogenase, the beans are poisonous. When they eat fava beans they get severe hemolytic anemia and they may die as a result. (Dr, 432) Symptoms are severe weakness, fainting and perhaps vomiting.
    FIRST AID: Administer oxygen if it is available. Take the patient to a physician.

Manihot esculenta Crantz (manioc, tapioca, cassava)
    Manioc is native to Brazil. The plant grows one to three meters (three to nine feet) tall. There are both variegated and all-green varieties. The leaves are palmately

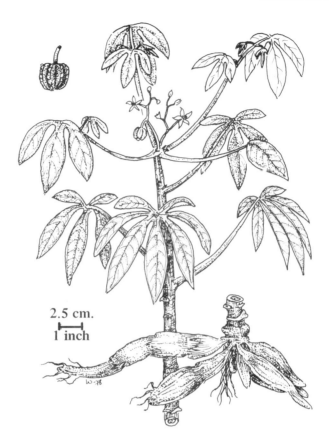

2.5 cm.
1 inch

MANIHOT ESCULENTA   Tapioca; Cassava; Manioc

divided, nearly to the base, into three to seven narrow, pointed divisions. The leaves are ten to twenty centimeters (four to eight inches) across. The flowers are small and inconspicuous. The fruits are globular, one centimeter (about half an inch) in diameter, with six narrow wings. Manioc is grown as an ornamental and for food throughout the tropics.

There is considerable variation in the toxicity of this plant. Some varieties are nontoxic while others are extremely toxic. They contain the same cyanogenic glycoside as the lima bean, linamarin. (ACS, 519; H, 118; K, 192)

The tubers are edible if properly cooked. To be sure (since you can't be sure that a given plant is free of toxin) they should be boiled for a long time and the water discarded. They may then be eaten like potatoes. The tubers are also a source of tapioca. In making tapioca the starch is removed by adding water to the crushed tubers, mixing thoroughly and allowing the starch to settle. The residue of the tubers is removed from the water and the starch is cooked. As it cooks the tiny balls characteristics of tapioca form.

Symptoms are those of cyanide poisoning. The person has vomiting and diarrhea. Breathing is first rapid, then irregular with gasping. The patient becomes excited and anxious (with good reason, for cyanide frequently kills). The skin, particularly the lips and fingertips, turns blue. Later symptoms include staggering, pa ralysis, convulsions and coma. Symptoms may appear rapidly. (K, 26; P&T, 128 ff.)

FIRST AID: Induce vomiting if it has not spontaneously occurred. Administer oxygen if it is available. Take the patient to a physician. Speed is essential, for cyanide is a rapid killer.

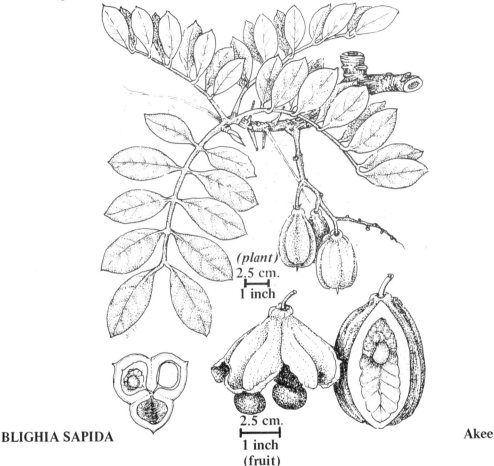

(plant)
2.5 cm.
1 inch

BLIGHIA SAPIDA

2.5 cm.
1 inch
(fruit)

Akee

Blighia sapida Koenig (akee, ackee)

Akee, a native of Guinea, Africa, is a handsome tree growing ten to fifteen meters (thirty to forty feet) high. It has dark green, pinnately compound leaves with six to ten oblong leaflets. The terminal leaflets are about fifteen centimeters (six inches) long, the inner ones progressively shorter. The flowers are five-parted, greenish or yellowish white. The fruit forms as a slightly elongate globe about eight centimeters (three inches) long with three small ridges. It later opens along these ridges to reveal three shiny black seeds on a cream-colored fleshy base (the aril).

Akee is extremely rare in Hawaii. (The only specimens I'm aware of are in Foster Botanical Gardens.) However, it deserves mention here because of the conflicting reports of its toxicity, and because its extreme popularity in Jamaica and the West Indies may make it more popular here. Toxicity of this plant has been reported in various references. (K, 217; H, 101; N, 536) However, C. Dennis Adams (Ad, 30) states that the fruit is eaten extensively in Jamaica and reports of poisonings are rare there.

Poisoning by akee may be avoided completely by taking some simple precautions. First of all, the fruit is poisonous only when the fruit is either unripe or overripe. Secondly the toxin (a complex amino acid, beta-methylenecyclopropylamine) is concentrated in the fibrous coat (raphe) and the seeds. The fleshy portion (aril) to which the seeds are attached is less toxic. Thirdly the toxin is quite soluble in water. Therefore, according to Adams, if the fruits are picked ripe, if the raphe and the seeds are first separated from the arils and thrown away, and if the arils are lightly boiled in water which is then discarded, then the arils are wholesome. The flavor is nutlike and Adams mentions that a favorite way of serving akee in Jamaica is with salt fish.

Symptoms are both delayed and abrupt, and they are more severe among people who are malnourished. Two to seventy hours after eating akee the patient suddenly vomits and rapidly goes into hypoglycemic coma.

FIRST AID: Take the patient to a physician. Speed is essential. If breathing has stopped be sure the breathing passages are open and apply artificial respiration.

Physalis peruviana L. (ground cherry, pohā)

Pohās are from South America. The plant is a perennial herb which grows in recently disturbed areas. Various sources report the unripe fruit to be toxic (A, 50; K, 287; H, 141) but I have eaten half-ripe pohās, both raw and as jam, without ill effects. Possibly the completely green fruit is toxic, but it is also bitter to the taste. The rest of the plant, especially the leaves, contains the steroid-glycosidal alkaloid, solanine. (See *Solanum*, below)

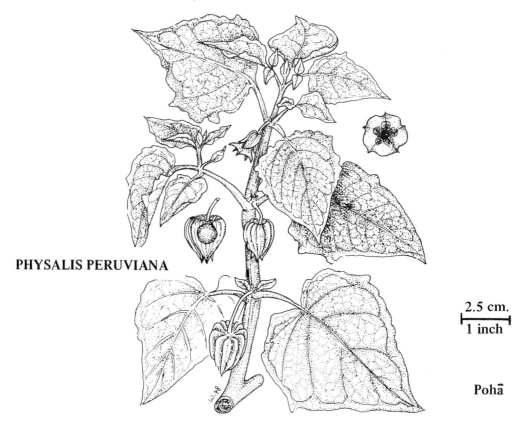

PHYSALIS PERUVIANA

2.5 cm.
1 inch

Pohā

Solanum spp. This is a large genus of plants from all over the world. It includes several familiar plants. The smallest are herbs. There are also vines, shrubs, woody vines and trees in this genus. The food-bearing species are these:

S. nigrum L., *S. nodiferum* Jacq. and *S. americanum* Mill. (Black nightshade, pōpolo) are treated by some botanists as one species. They are certainly difficult to distinguish in the field. Pōpolo is an herb to 0.6 meter (two feet) high, with white flowers and small, black, delicious-tasting berries. Like pohās, pōpolos grow wild in disturbed areas throughout Hawaii. Kingsbury (K, 290) reports cases of poisoning by this plant in the mainland and Arnold (A, 55) lists it as "dangerous at best." However, I have eaten the berries without ill effects, and so have many other Islanders. It may be that our Hawaiian varieties are safe, or it may be that our climate or soil render the plants grown here nontoxic. (cf. *Digitalis*, p. 63) The leaves are toxic, One never knows, of course, when some toxic varieties may be introduced.

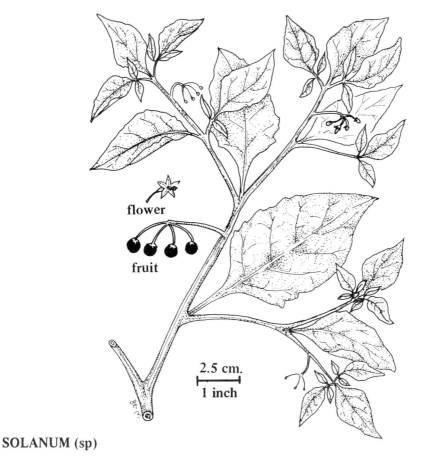

flower

fruit

2.5 cm.
1 inch

SOLANUM (sp)   Pōpolo

S. melongena L. (eggplant) is a common garden vegetable from southeastern Asia. The large, blackish fruit is edible, but the other parts of the plants are toxic, containing solanine.

S. tuberosum L. (potato), from the Andes, has edible tubers. If the tubers are exposed to light for a few days they turn green. These green parts and the sprouts from potatoes are poisonous, but if they are removed from the tubers the rest is safe to eat. The leaves and stems are poisonous. (K, 293)

The toxin of *Solanum* spp. is the glycosidal-steroid alkaloid, solanine. This can be broken down into two substances: a toxic steroid alkaloid (solanidine) and a sugar (solanose). Solanine is found only in the family Solanaceae, and it is found in many species of the family. The toxicity of *Solanum* species varies from one species to another and from one plant to another in the same species. Different parts of the plants may also vary in toxicity. The range is from nontoxic to a toxic dose of 1.0 mg/kg of body weight. (A, 53; H, 141; K, 287; Q, 141)

Symptoms are as variable as the toxicity: apathy, drowsiness, salivation, difficulty in breathing, trembling, weakness, paralysis, vomiting and diarrhea or constipation.

FIRST AID: Induce vomiting if it has not already occurred. Do not attempt to check spontaneous vomiting or diarrhea. Consult a physician.

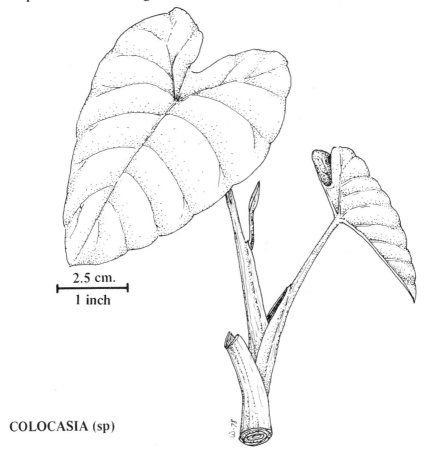

2.5 cm.

1 inch

COLOCASIA (sp)   Taro

Colocasia esculenta (L.) Schott (taro) and *Alocasia cucullata* (Lour.) G. Don (Chinese taro) are originally from eastern Asia. Taro was brought in by the Hawaiians. The plants look very similar to other species of *Colocasia, Alocasia* and *Caladium* which may be more toxic. All of these plants contain varying amounts of calcium oxalate, which must be removed by cooking. Both the corms and leaves are edible. If eaten raw they cause the characteristic burning, stinging sensation in the mouth

They are safe to eat when cooked, for heat destroys or removes oxalates. (However, see the other entry for *Colocasia* and *Caladium* on p. 64)

Allium cepa L. (onion) from Persia, *A. sativum* L. (garlic) and *A. schoenoprasm* L. (chives) from Asia, are common vegetables and flavorings. They contain uncharacterized alkaloids which cause hemolytic anemia. The toxic dose to dogs is 5 gm/kg body weight. (K, 446) If the same dosage is toxic to man anything in excess of 350 grams (two three-inch onions) might cause symptoms. Few people are likely to eat this much at one time.

Dioscorea bulbifera L. (common yam, air potato, hoi).
      This is the true yam. It is native to tropical Asia and it was brought in by the Hawaiians. It has heart-shaped to ovate leaves, alternate at the base of the plant and opposite further up. There are both aerial and underground tubers. Yam tubers are similar to sweet potatoes in both flavor and preparation, but they are not related. Most of the "yams" sold in grocery stores are actually sweet potatoes, which are a species of *Ipomoea* (p. 95)
      True yams contain a glucoside which is easily destroyed by heat. Various sources (N, 236; A, 33; D1, fam. 73; Q, 178) mention that raw yams are poisonous, causing nausea and vomiting when eaten. Heating destroys the toxin, so cooked yams are safe to eat. In any case, they are not very poisonous and they are their own antidote, since the vomiting removes the poison. They are mentioned here mainly to dispel any fears one might have about them.

FOOD PLANTS WITH OTHER POISONOUS PARTS

Annona muricata L. (soursop), *A. reticulata* L. (custard apple, bullock's heart) and *A. squamosa* L. (sweetsop) are all from tropical America. They are grown in Hawaii for their delicious, edible fruits, but the bark contains the aporphine alkaloids, muricine and 5,6-dioxyaporphine. Eating the bark (admittedly unlikely, except for small children) causes diarrhea. (Q, 306)

Rheum rhaponticum L. (rhubarb)
      Rhubarb is native to Siberia. It is occasionally grown in Hawaii as a vegetable, but it does well only at higher elevations. The petioles are edible, commonly used in pies. However, the leaf blades are toxic, containing large amounts of soluble oxalates. Kingsbury (K, 230) cites several cases, including death, of people being poisoned by eating rhubarb leaves. The symptoms are those of oxalate poisoning: nausea, vomiting, weakness, difficulty in breathing, burning sensation in the mouth and throat, internal bleeding and coma. (H, 76)
      FIRST AID: Induce vomiting if it has not already occurred. Take the patient to a physician.

Passiflora spp. (passion fruit, passion flower, liliko'i, banana poka)
      Passion fruits come from tropical America. Many species of them are grown in Hawaii, both cultivated and wild. The best known species here are *P. edulis* Sims (liliko'i) and *P. mollissima* (H.B.K.) Bailey (banana poka). The juicy flesh around the seeds and the seeds themselves are edible, but the leaves and hull of the fruits may contain as much as two grams of hydrocyanic acid per kilogram fresh weight in the form of a cyanogenic glycoside. (Q, 630) Since the lethal dose of cyanide may be as low as 0.7 mg/kg body weight (PT, 138), the lethal dose of fresh plant parts may be as little as 0.35 gm/kg body weight. No human deaths have been reported but this

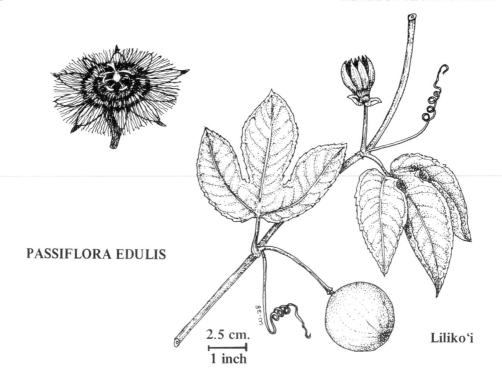

PASSIFLORA EDULIS

2.5 cm.
1 inch

Liliko'i

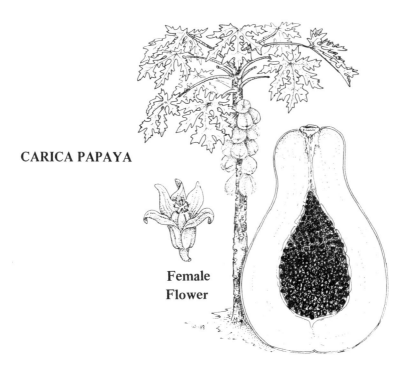

CARICA PAPAYA

Female
Flower

Papaya

plant is potentially dangerously poisonous, especially to small children (who may put anything into their mouths). The symptoms are those of cyanide poisoning. (See *Manihot* p. 70).

FIRST AID: Induce vomiting even if you only suspect that a person has eaten the poisonous parts. Take the patient to a physician. Administer oxygen if it is available and if the patient shows symptoms.

Carica papaya L. (papaya)

Papayas are native to Brazil. Papaya fruits are delicious and highly nutritious but the milky sap from any part of the plant irritates the skin. The irritation is probably due to the enzyme papain, which digests proteins, including the skin. (Q, 632) Symptoms are reddening of the skin and intense itching. Wash any sap or affected areas with cold, clear water. The symptoms quickly disappear.

Prunus spp. (cherry, apricot, almond, peach, plum)

These are all familiar fruits from Europe, Asia and North America. The kernels of the pits of these fruits contain the cyanogenic glycoside, amygdalin. Cyanide poisoning from eating the seed kernels of these fruits is stated by Kingsbury to be one of the commonest kinds of plant poisonings in the United States. (K, 365) Eating raw kernels is treacherous at best. Amygdalin is not toxic unless it is broken down. Depending upon the particular bacteria in the person's digestive tract, the substance may or may not be broken down. Different plants of the same species may also vary in toxicity (e.g., sweet almonds are a nontoxic variety developed from the very toxic bitter almond). Therefore a person may "get by" many times without symptoms after eating the kernels only to become poisoned at another time. (ACS, 519; H, 79) Symptoms are those of cyanide poisoning. (See *Manihot*, p. 70).

FIRST AID: Induce vomiting if it has not already occurred. Administer oxygen if it is available. Take the patient to a physician immediately. Speed is essential, for cyanide is a rapid-acting poison.

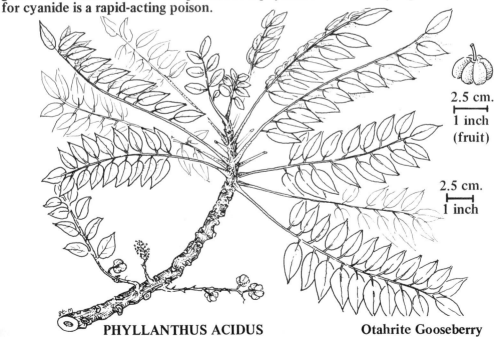

2.5 cm.
1 inch
(fruit)

2.5 cm.
1 inch

PHYLLANTHUS ACIDUS   **Otahrite Gooseberry**

Phyllanthus acidus (L.) Skeels (Otaheite gooseberry) is occasionally grown in Hawaii. The fruit is edible but other parts, including the pits, are purgative (Q, 495) The only precaution one needs to take under normal eating is to spit out the pits.

Pyrus communis L. (pear) and *P. malus* L. (apple) are good to eat but the seeds contain amygdalin. A man was killed by eating a cupful of apple seeds (K, 365) but one will not be poisoned by the number of seeds he will encounter in eating apples or pears.

Anacardium occidentale L. (cashew)

Cashews are native to the West Indies. The "nut" we eat is nontoxic, but the rest of the plant contains oils similar to those of poison ivy (*Toxicodendron* spp.). See *Mangifera*, below.

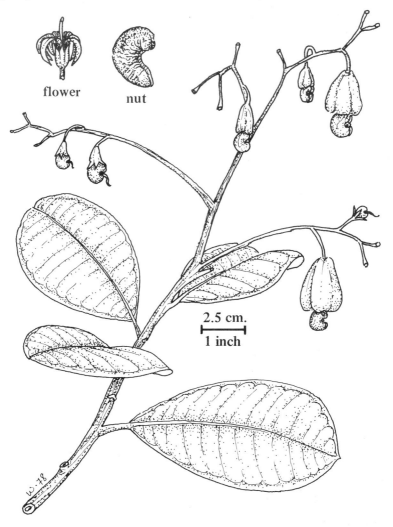

flower   nut

2.5 cm.
1 inch

ANACARDIUM OCCIDENTALE   **Flower Nut Cashew**

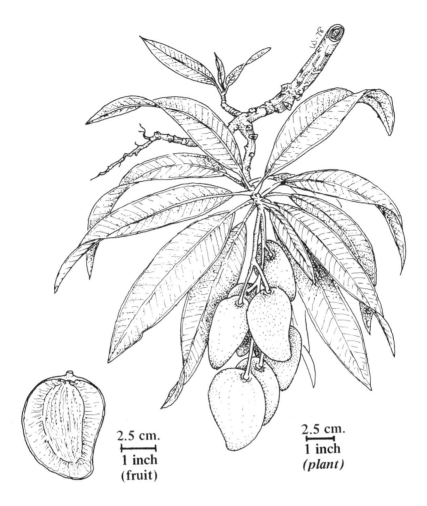

2.5 cm.
|—————|
1 inch
(fruit)

2.5 cm.
|—————|
1 inch
(plant)

MANGIFERA INDICA   **Mango**

Mangifera indica L. (mango)
      Mangoes come from southeastern Asia. Most people can eat the fruit and handle the plant without symptoms. However, since they have the same or similar oils to those of poison ivy *(Toxicodendron* spp.) some people get similar symptoms: reddening and blistering of the skin. Dr. Harry Arnold Jr. of Straub Clinic in Honolulu has recorded the interesting observation that people reared in Hawaii or Puerto Rico, where mangoes are common, seldom contract symptoms from poison ivy when they move to the mainland. He speculates that this may be due to immunization by repeated contact with the lesser amounts of the irritant oils in mangoes.

Lycopersicon esculentum Mill. (tomato)
      Tomatoes are from western South America. When my grandmother was a child tomatoes were called "love apples" and they were considered poisonous. Tomato fruits are good to eat, of course, but the leaves and stems contain the steroidglycosidal alkaloid, solanine. See *Solanum*, p. 73.

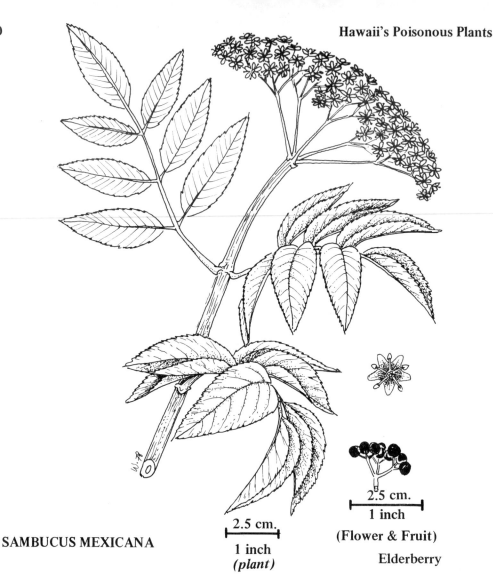

SAMBUCUS MEXICANA

2.5 cm.
1 inch
(plant)

2.5 cm.
1 inch
(Flower & Fruit)
Elderberry

Sambucus mexicana Presl. (elderberry)

The eldberries growing in Hawaii are from Central America. They are closely related to the species growing in the mainland and anyone knowing mainland elderberries will recognize those growing here. It grows as a shrub up to five meters (fifteen feet) high. It has dark green, pinnately compound leaves with five to nine leaflets. The globe-shaped corymbs of tiny flowers are intensely white. The fruit, a berry about five millimeters in diameter, is green when unripe, ripening to black or dark purple.

Elderberry fruits are edible, though they may cause stomach upset if eaten green or raw. They are well known as a fruit for wine. The other parts of the plant are toxic. A cyanogenic glycoside, sambunigrin, is present in the plant (ACS, 519), but the main cause of symptoms is a purgative and emetic substance whose chemical nature is unknown. It is sufficiently toxic to cause symptoms in children who use the freshly cut stems as blowguns. (K, 389)

FIRST AID: Induce vomiting if it has not already occurred. Take the patient to a physician if the symptoms persist or are severe.

CHAPTER V: TYPES OF POISONS IN PLANTS

The toxins of most of the plants in this book are known and they usually fall into one or more of the following categories: phytotoxins, glycosides, alkaloids, phenols, toxic resins, oxalates, purgative oils, isothiocyanates (mustard oils), photosensitizers and hypoglycemic substances. The first eight of these categories are chemical and the last two are symptomatic categories.

PHYTOTOXINS (Dr, 431; K, 37; Q, 358; 512; 529)

The phytotoxins are proteins very similar both chemically and physiologically to the bacterial toxins. They are among the most toxic substances known to Ricin, the toxin of Ricinus (p. 20), requires only seven micrograms to kill an adult human. These toxins are albumins or globulins very similar to the toxins of the bacterium, *Clostridium botulinum*, which is responsible for the usually fatal food poisoning, botulism. As with botulin, the symptoms of phytotoxin poisoning are slow in starting, often taking one or two days to develop. These toxins attack the central nervous system, causing such symptoms as diplopia (double vision), dizziness, difficulty in swallowing and general weakness. Some of the phytotoxins are highly irritant to the gastrointestional tract and these cause vomiting and diarrhea, with or without bleeding. Some also destroy blood cells (hemolysis and agglutination). Death usually occurs by respiratory failure. Recovery, when it occurs, is quite slow, often taking months for the patient to return to full health. Once symptoms occur there are no antidotes for these toxins -- treatment can be only symptomatic and palliative.

Even if a phytotoxin is not itself irritant it is frequently accompanied in the plant by saponins (below) or purgative oils (p.86). An example is *Ricinus communis,* which contains ricin and castor oil. These cause vomiting and diarrhea. Because different substances cause the various symptoms, the symptoms do not occur simultaneously. Often a patient will appear to be recovering satisfactorily from the gastrointestional symptoms (e.g., from castor oil) only to succumb later to the phytotoxins.

Because the phytotoxins are invariably very toxic any plant containing them must be considered dangerously toxic.

Phytotoxins are found throughout the plant kingdom, but they are particularly prevalent in the families Euphorbiaceae (p. 91) and Leguminosae (p. 90).

GLYCOSIDES

Glycosides are substances which include a sugar molecule in their chemical structures. Some glycosides consist entirely of sugars (e.g., sucrose, lactose and cellulose) and these are usually nontoxic. Other glycosides can be hydrolyzed into sugar and non-sugar (aglycone) units. The aglycones of the toxic glycosides are either complex organic substances or simpler organic substances containing the cyanide (nitrile) radical, which can in turn be hydrolyzed to yield hydrocyanic acid.

Saponins: (K, 32) The saponins are all glycosides capable of lowering the surface tension of water and thus making the water easily foamed. (The name "saponin" is derived from the Latin word for soap.) Some plants contain large amounts of saponins. Suspensions of material from these plants are sometimes excellent detergents. Common names of such plants include soapwort, soapberry, soap root and soap plant (all names applied to more than one species), and they have been used by man as cleansing agents. Until the advent of synthetic detergents they were often used in preference to soap because they worked well in hard water.

When injected into the bloodstream saponins are always very toxic. The surface active properties of saponins cause hemolysis (breakdown of the blood cells) and damage to nervous tissue. However, the intact human intestinal tract is impervious to saponins, so most saponins do not poison people who eat them in plants. It is only when the saponin is irritant to the gastrointestinal irritants, that these substances gain entry into the bloodstream and poison a person.

All saponins are glycosides but there are two types of saponins; triterpenoid and steroid saponins. The symptoms produced by both types of saponins are similar since they are caused by surface active properties rather than specific chemical reactions.

Cardiac glycosides: (Dr, 332; K, 30) Another group of glycosides are invariably toxic, and these are called "cardiac glycosides" because of their action of the heart. They all have steroid aglycone units of a fairly specific chemical structure:

OLEANDRIN, found in Nerium spp.
The cardiac stimulation is associated with the circled portions.

This structure seems to be responsible for the cardiac activity but the mode of action is unclear. The specific symptoms produced by the cardiac glycosides vary somewhat from plant to plant but a typical reaction is that of digitalin (p. 63). In carefully controlled doses some of these glycosides (particularly digitalin) are extremely useful drugs, for they can be used to strengthen and stabilize the action of the heart.

Cardiac glycosides are found in many species, most of them in the families Apocynaceae (p. 91) , Scrophulariaceae (p. 92) and Liliaceae (p. 93).

Cyanogenic glycosides: (ACS, 519; Dr, 221; K, 23; PT, 128) These are glycosides containing the cyanide (nitrile) radical which can be released from the molecule to yield hydrocyanic acid. The symptoms of cyanide poisoning are well known and they are described on p. 70.

Considerable controversy has arisen over the toxicity of plants containing cyanogenic glycosides. For example, apricot kernels have been promoted as a "health food," but they are prohibited by the Federal Food and Drug Administration to be sold as a food, because of their potential toxicity. This controversy has happened because the human digestive tract does not always break down the glycosides to yield hydrocyanic acid. The digestive tract is not of itself capable of breaking down the glycosides, so the release of cyanide requires some decay of the plant material or activity of the intestinal flora of the person eating the plant. There are also wide variations between individual plants of the same species, or even within a single plant at different times, in the amount of cyanogenic glycosides they contain. Because of these factors a person may eat fairly large quantities of cyanophoric plants without ill effects, only to have severe symptoms or to die from eating small portions of the same plant at another time. At best the well-known cyanophoric plants are treacherous.

Cyanogenic glycosides are widely distributed throughout the plant kingdom. Such widely diverse species as *Prunus persica* (p. 77), *Phaseolus lunatus* (p. 68), *Sorghum* spp. (p. 93), *Linum* spp. (p. 91) and *Manihot esculentum* (p. 70) all contain cyanides. A complete list would include thousands of species, though most of them contain only traces of cyanide.

ALKALOIDS

(ACS, 473; K, 18; Dr and PT under the names of various alkaloids) Alkaloids are generally named after plants in which they are found. Thus atropine is named after *Atropa belladonna*, solanine and solanidine after *Solanum* spp., cocaine after *Erythoxylum coca*, and so on. Thus, though an alkaloid's name may say something about its source it really tells us nothing about its chemistry, physiological effects and toxicology. Therefore it is customary also to classify them on the basis of their chemical structure. This is done in this book: whenever possible each alkaloid is introduced with a statement of a chemical substance to which it is related and the name of the specific alkaloid. Examples: the pyridine alkaloid, nicotine; the isoquinoline alkaloid, sanguinarine. The chemical groupings for the alkaloids mentioned in this book are the following:

aporphine	indole
isoquinoline	pyridine
pyrrolizidine	steroid-glycosidal
tropane	polycyclic diterpenoid

(Colchicine belongs to a special category and it is discussed on (p. 66).

However, this still does not tell us about the toxicological or physiological effects of the alkaloids. Alkaloids similar chemically usually have similar effects on humans, but in some cases they have very different effects. Protopine and morphine are both isoquinoline alkaloids, but protopine, though highly toxic, does not show the addicting and narcotic effects of morphine. Atropine is related chemically to cocaine, but atropine is a muscle relaxant and paralytic while cocaine is a local anesthetic and addicting, central nervous system stimulant. This is not to say that chemically related alkaloids never have similar effects - codeine and morphine are similar both chemically and physiologically - it only means that each alkaloid is unique in its toxicology and symptomology and chemical similarity can be used only as a general guide.

One particular group of alkaloids deserves special mention: the glycosidal-steroid alkaloids of the family Solanaceae. The most important of these are solanine and its aglycone, solanidine:

SOLANINE

They could be listed in this chapter either as alkaloids or steroid glycosides, for they are both. They are similar in their action to the saponins, although they provoke other symptoms as well. (See *Solanum*, p. 73).

PHENOLS (ACS, 497; K, 213; Q, 212)

These are substances of widely varying chemical structures, but they are all related to phenol ("carbolic acid"). Many of them, like phenol itself, are highly irritant. Best known of the phenols is 3-n-pentadecylcatechol, the toxin of poison ivy. Unlike many irritants it is slow in showing symptoms, usually taking two or three days to develop, and it affects only some people. The toxin is not volatile so direct contact with it is essential to provoke symptoms. However, direct contact may be through pets, clothing, tolls and other people, so a person does not need to handle the plant itself to contract symptoms. Unfortunately there is not much that can be done to prevent symptoms once a sensitive person contacts one of these plants, even though there is a delay in the onset of symptoms. Apparently the toxin combines immediately with skin proteins, so washing with soap or detergents is of help only to prevent spreading of the toxin to other parts of the body. Desentization by contact with very small amounts of the toxin may be accomplished *before any contact*, but this must be done under careful medical supervision. We do not have poison ivy in Hawaii but we do have other plants of the same family (Anacardiaceae) with the same or similar toxins: *Anacardium* (p. 78), *Mangifera indica* (p. 79) and *Semecarpus anacardium* (p. 91).. Occasionally people contract dermatitis from these plants.

Another plant, *Grevillea banksii* (p. 43) causes similar symptoms, but the chemical nature of the toxin is unknown. The toxin is apparently not related to that of the Anacardiaceae, for sensitivity to Grevillea does not correlate with sensitivity to Anacardiaceae (Harry Arnold Jr., M.D., personal comm.)

Some phenols are not particularly irritant but provoke other symptoms. The stimulants in *Piper betle* (Q, 212) are phenolic and so are the tranquilizing substances in *P. methysticum* (ACS, 508; 533). The oils in *P. nigrum* (black pepper, the spice) are phenolic and irritant, but the effects are immediate and not at all like those of poison ivy. (The sneezing one does in reaction to pepper is a reaction to irritation.) It is interesting that all three of these plants belong to the same genus, have chemically similar substances and yet have very different effects.

RESINS (K, 36)

Resins are common in plants. "Resin" is a general term for non-nitrogenous, a-morphous (non-crystalline) substances of complex chemical structure. As the structures are determined they are often reclassified under more specific categories. Many resins are nontoxic (e.g., the resins in tea), while others have varying effects on man. The resins important to us are those of *Rhododendron* (p. 38), *Melia* (p. 48), and *Calotropis* (p. 56), all of which are irritant.

OXALATES (Dr, 171; K, 33; PT, 64)

Salts of oxalic acid are found in many plants. All base their toxicity primarily on the tendency of calcium oxalate to precipitate from solution. Only sodium, potassium and calcium oxalates are common in plants. Calcium oxalate is distinguished from the other salts by its markedly different symptoms, so oxalates are generally described toxicologically as two group: calcium oxalate (raphides) and soluble oxalates.

Calcium oxalate varies considerably in its solubility in water, depending upon the acidity of the solution. It tends to be more·soluble in acid than basic solutions. It easily precipitates as needle-like crystals which, if they form in cells, can penetrate the cell membranes. Many investigators feel that this action is responsible for the intense irritation of the mouth which happens when a person puts plants of the family Araceae (p. 64) into the mouth. (Other investigators dispute this, attributing the symptoms to other effects of calcium oxalate.) In any case the symptoms are characteristic: intense irritation of the mucosa, resulting in reddening, swelling and burning pain in the mouth and throat. Since the effects are immediate and excruciating people are not likely to ingest enough calcium oxalate to cause dangerous poisoning.

Soluble oxalates are more insidious. They can be eaten in toxic quantities before symptoms appear. Their toxicity is also based on the variable solubility of calcium oxalate in water, but since they are initially soluble they enter the blood stream. Their activity is two fold. First of all they reduce the amount of calcium ions in the blood, sometimes to dangerously low levels, because the oxalate ion has a strong affinity to calcium. This upsets the metabolism of cells, since they need calcium, and it also disrupts the body's control of the acidity of the blood. As important toxicologically is the tendency for calcium oxalate to precipitate in the kidneys. Precipitation of this substance in the kidney cells can cause their destruction just as it does the oral mucosa. Crystals also form in the lumens of the tubules, clogging them and preventing normal kidney activity.

PURGATIVE OILS (references under the various plants)

Any oil, taken in large quantities, can cause diarrhea but some oils cause diarrhea by provoking irritation of the intestinal tract. Milder among these are the oil of *Aleurites* (p. 44) and castor oil (p. 20). Some of the highly irritant oils are pinhoen oil, found in *Jatropha* spp. (p. 15) and croton oil. (Croton oil is not found in any plants in Hawaii. The "crotons" grown here are of another genus and not especially toxic.) These oils are quite complex chemically and some appear to have resinous fractions.

ISOTHIOCYANATES (MUSTARD OILS)
(K, 28; ACS, 483)

Isothiocyanates are found in the family Cruciferae (p. 89). The two commonest are allyl isothiocyanate and 3-butenyl isothiocyanate. When applied to the skin they cause reddening and blistering, with a warm, hot or burning sensation. The "hot" taste of mustard is due to these chemicals. Taken internally they can cause irritation of the gastrointestinal tract, with diarrhea, vomiting and abdominal pain. The isothiocyanates also cause hemolysis (breakdown of the red blood corpuscles) with resulting anemia. Thus it is recommended that people limit their diet of cabbages, radishes, turnips and mustard, although they are wholesome in the amounts usually eaten by Americans. (These plants also contain substances which cause goiter, again only when eaten to excess.)

PHOTOSENSITIZERS (K, 52)

Some substances found in plants cause an animal or human to become highly sensitive to sunlight. This sensitization includes both an increased tendency to sunburn and dazzling of the eyes. The hypersensitivity is due to substances which are capable of absorbing light and transferring the energy to the surrounding tissues. There are two types of photosensitizers of plant origin: the primary photosensitizers and the hepatogenic photosensitizers.

Primary photosensitizers: Some plants, notably *Hypericum* and *Ammi* have substances in them which are capable of absorbing light. (Neither of these two genera are common in Hawaii.) When these plants are eaten the substances are absorbed and carried through the bloodstream to the skin and eyes. These plants are known as primary photosensitizers because they cause direct photosensitization without alteration in the organs of the body.

Hepatogenic photosensitizers: Other plants (e.g., *Lantana*, (p. 62) cause photosensitization indirectly. They contain no photodynamic substances which can be absorbed by the body as such. However, they have substances which disrupt liver function. The normal liver excretes through the bile duct some substances accumulated as by-products of metabolism. Among these are some photodynamic substances. If normal excretion from the liver is prevented these substances go into the bloodstream, which carries them to the skin and the retina of the eye. The photosensitizers are toxic mainly because they damage the liver, and as liver poisons they are much more dangerous than the primary photosensitizers.

Mode of action of the photosensitizers: With both the primary and hepatogenic photosensitizers a photodynamic substance in the skin or retina absorbs light and somehow transmits this energy to nearby tissues. The result is sunburn and associated symptoms of the skin and dazzling of vision. Dark-skinned people and animals are less susceptible to the photosensitizers than light-skinned ones, since they have pigmentation which screens out light necessary to produce symptoms.

HYPOGLYCEMIC SUBSTANCES (ACS, 494; K, 217; Q, 639)

These are substances which cause lowering of blood sugar. They do not constitute a single chemical group. The way in which they reduce blood sugar is not understood. It may be by inhibiting or destroying the enzymes necessary for releasing sugar into the blood. According to Quisumbing the hypoglycemic substance in *Lagerstroemia* (p. 41) may operate in the same manner as insulin. Since the substances are not chemically similar it is possible that each operates in a different manner.

APPENDIX A: CHECKLIST OF POISONOUS PLANTS IN HAWAII

This checklist includes all of the plants in Hawaii which have been implicated in human poisoning by the scientific literature. Names of plants discussed in this book are followed by numbers. Names of plants not discussed in this book are followed by numbers in parenthesis referring to literature in which the plants are discussed. Complete listing of the references is in the Bibliography. (Plants not covered by this book are either uncommon in Hawaii or not very poisonous.)

The taxonomic system used in this book is that of Cronquist, as described in *The Evolution and Classification of Flowering Plants*; Houghton-Mifflin Co. (Boston) 1968. The only deviation from his system is the segregation of Liliaceae and Amaryllidaceae into separate families. This was done because these have been heretofore universally been described as separate families.

CLASS: DICOTYLEDONAE
Subclass: Magnoliidae
ORDER: MAGNOLIALES
Family: Annonaceae

Annona muricata L. (soursop) 75
A. reticulata L. (custard apple, bullock's heart) 75
A. squamosa L. (sweetsop) 75

Family: Myristicaceae

Myristica fragrans Houtt. (nutmeg) 67

Family: Lauraceae

Cassytha filiformis L. (kauna'oa) (Q, 318)

Family: Hernandiaceae

Hernandia sonora L. (hernandia) (Q, 328)

ORDER: PIPERALES
Family: Piperaceae

Piper betle L. (betel pepper) (Q, 212)
P. methysticum Frost. f. ('awa, kava) (ACS, 508; 533)

ORDER: RANUNCULALES
Family: Ranunculaceae

Anemone hupehensis Lem. & Lem. f. (Japanese anemone) 33
Delphinium spp. (delphinium, larkspur) 34
Ranunculus spp. (ranunculus, buttercup) (K, 140)

Family: Berberidaceae

Nandina domestica Thunb. (sacred bamboo, Japanese fire bush) (ACS, 519)

ORDER: PAPAVERALES
Family: Papaveraceae

Argemone glauca (Nutt. ex Prain) Pope (Hawaiian poppy, pua-kala) 11
Papaver somniferum L. (opium poppy) 35

Subclass: Hamamelidae
ORDER: URTICALES
Family: Moraceae

Antiaris toxicaria Lesch. (upas tree) (A, 27; Q, 224)
Streblus asper Lour. (Siamese rough bush) (Q, 242)

Family: Urticaceae

Hesperocnide sandwicensis Wedd. (N, 316)
Urtica urens L. (nettle) (N, 316)

Subclass: Caryophyllidae
ORDER: CARYOPHYLLALES
Family: Phytolaccaceae

Phytolacca spp. (pokeweed) 35
Rivinia humilis L. (rouge plant, coral berry) 36

Family: Nyctaginaceae

Boerhavia diffusa L. (alena) (Q, 273)
Mirabilis jalapa L. (four o'clock, marvel of Peru, pua ahiahi) (A, 47; H, 74; O, 73; Q, 275)

Family: Caryophyllaceae

Drymaria cordata (L.) Willd. (drymary) 37

Family: Chenopodiaceae

Beta vulgaris L. (beet, chard) 67
Spinacia oleracea L. (spinach) 67

ORDER: POLYGONALES
Family: Polygonaceae

Rheum rhaponticum L. (rhubarb) 75
Rumex acetosella L. (dock, sorrel) (K, 231; Q, 259; H, 15)
R. crispus L. (dock, sorrel) (K, 231; Q, 259; H, 15)

ORDER: PLUMBAGINALES
Family: Plumbaginaceae

Plumbago spp. (plumbago, 'ilie'e) (A, 51; H, 15; Q, 695)

Subclass: Dilleniidae
ORDER: DILLENIALES
Family: Dilleniaceae

Dillenia indica L. and D. philippinensis Rolfe (dillenia) (Q, 612)

ORDER: THEALES
Family: Guttiferae (Clusiaceae)

Calophyllum inophyllum L. (kamani) (Q, 616)
Hypericum perforatum L. (St. Johnswort) 37

ORDER: MALVALES
Family: Tiliaceae

Corchorus capsularis L. (jute) (Q, 564)

Family: Sterculiaceae

Kleinhovia hospita L. (guest tree) (Q, 604)

ORDER: LECYTHIDALES
Family: Lecythidaceae

Barringtonia asiatica (L.) Kurz (fish poison tree) (A, 30; Q, 1043)

ORDER: VIOLALES
Family: Violaceae

Viola odorata L. (violet) (Q, 624)

Family: Passifloraceae

Passiflora spp. (passion fruit, liliko'i, poka) 75

Family: Caricaceae

Carica papaya L. (papaya) 76

Family: Cucurbitaceae

Luffa acuangula (L.) Roxb. (dishcloth gourd, seequa) (Q, 940)
Momordica charantia L. (bitter gourd, bitter melon, balsam apple, balsam pear) 67

ORDER: CAPPARALES
Family: Capparidaceae

Gynandropsis gynandra (L.) Merr. (spider flower, honohina) (Q, 342)

Family: Cruciferae (Brassicaceae)

Amoracia rusticana (Lam.) Gaertn. (horseradish) 68
Brassica spp. (cabbage, mustard, cauliflower, broccoli, kale, turnip, Brussel sprouts) 68
Raphanus raphinastrum L. (charlock) 68
Raphanus sativus L. (radish) 68

ORDER: PRIMULALES
Family: Primulaceae

Anagallis arvensis L. (scarlet pimpernel, weatherglass) (H, 12; K, 250)

ORDER: ERICALES
Family: Ericaceae

Rhododendron indicum (L.) Sweet (azalea) 38

ORDER: EBENALES
Family: Sapotaceae
Calocarpum sapota (Jacq.) Merr. (red sapote) (Q, 698)
Family: Ebenaceae
Diospyros ebenaster Retz (black sapote) (Q, 704)
Subclass: Rosidae
ORDER: ROSALES
Family: Saxifragaceae
Hydrangea macrophylla Ser. (hydrangea) 39
Family: Rosaceae
Prunus spp. (cherry, peach, apricot, almond, plum) 77
Pyrus spp. (apple, pear) 78
Family: Leguminosae (Fabaceae)
Abrus precatorius L. (jequirity bean, rosary pea) 13
Caesalpinia gilliesii Wall. ex Hook. (dwarf poinciana) (Q, 369)
C. pulcherrima (L.) Sw. (pride of Barbados) (Q, 369)
Clitorea terneata L. (butterfly pea) (Q, 387)
Crotalaria spp. (rattlepod, rattle box) 40
Cytisis scoparius (L.) Link (Scotch broom) (K, 320; ACS, 473)
Dolichos lablab L. (lablab bean, hyacinth bean) 69
Entada phaseoloides (L.) Merr. (St. Thomas bean) (Q, 399)
Lathyrus odoratus L. (vetch) (ACS, 473; 492; H, 85; K, 326)
Lupinus spp. (lupine, bluebonnet) (ACS, 473; 533; K, 333)
Pachyrrizus erosus (L.) Urb. (chopsui potato, yam bean, sargott) (Q, 416)
Phaseolus limensis Macf. and P. lunatus (lima bean) 68
Pueraria lobata (Willd.) Ohwi (kudzu, fan-kot) (Q, 427)
Robinia pseudoacacia L. (black locust) (H, 87; K, 351)
Sophora tomentosa L. (silver bush) (Q, 432)
Vicia faba L. (fava bean, broadbean) 69
V. sativa L. and V. villosa Roth (vetch) (K, 362)
Wisteria sinensis Sweet (wisteria) (H, 89; K, 364)
ORDER: MYRTALES
Family: Lythraceae
Lagerstroemia indica L. (crape myrtle, queen flower) 41
L. speciosa (L.) Pers. (giant crape myrtle) 41
Family: Thymeliaceae

Wikstroemia spp. ('akia) 42
Family: Myrtaceae
Eugenia cuminii (L.) Druce (Java plum) (Q, 667)
E. jambos L. (rose apple) (Q, 667)
ORDER: PROTEALES
Family: Proteaceae
Grevillea banksii R. Br. (kahili flower) 43
ORDER: CORNALES
Family: Rhizophoraceae
Rhizophora mucronata Lam. (mangrove) (Q, 652)
ORDER: CELASTRALES
Family: Aquifoliaceae
Ilex spp. (holly) (H, 95)
Family: Celastraceae
Euonymus japonicus L. f. (euonymous, burning bush, spindle tree) (H, 95; K, 208)
ORDER: EUPHORBIALES
Family: Buxaceae
Buxus sempervirens L. (common box) (H, 77; K, 197)

Family: Euphorbiaceae

Acalypha indica L. (acalypha) (Q, 490)
Aleurites fordii Hemsl. (tung oil tree) (H, 112; K, 182; Q, 491)
A. moluccana (L.) Will. (kukui, candlenut tree) 44
A. montana (Lour.) Wils. (Q, 491)
A. trisperma Blanco (banucalad) (Q, 491)
Antidesma bunius (L.) Spreng (bignay) (Q, 494)
Euphorbia spp. (spurges) 45
Excoecaria cochinchinensis Lour. (picara) ref: Paul Weissich
Hura crepitans L. (sandbox tree) (A, 41; H, 117; K, 190)
Jatropha spp. (jatropha, physic nut, coral plant) 15
Manihot esculenta Crantz (manioc, tapioca, cassava) 70
Pedilanthus tithimaloides (L.) Poit. (slipper flower, redbird cactus) 47
Phyllanthus acidus (L.) Skeels (Otaheite gooseberry) 78
Ricinus communis L. (castor bean) 20

ORDER: RHAMNALES
Family: Rhamnaceae

Rhamnus alaternus L. (buckthorn) (ACS, 507; K, 221)
Zizyphus mauritana Lam. (jujube) (Q, 557)

ORDER: SAPINDALES
Family: Sapindaceae

Blighia sapida Koenig (akee, ackee) 71

Family: Anacardiaceae

Anacardium occidentale L. (cashew) 78
Mangifera indica L. (mango) 79
Semecarpus anacardium L. (marking nut tree) (A, 54; ACS, 504; Q, 542)

Family: Simaroubaceae

Samadera indica Gaertn. (samadera) (Q, 474)

Family: Meliaceae

Lansium Domesticum Correa (langsat, lansone) (Q, 480)
Melia azedarach L. (pride of India, chinaberry) 48

ORDER: GERANIALES
Family: Oxalidaceae

Oxalis spp. (oxalis, sorrel) (K, 33; 200)

ORDER: LINALES
Family: Erythroxylaceae

Erythroxylum coca Lam. (coca, cocaine plant) 49

Family: Linaceae

Linum usitatissimum L. (flax, linen, linseed) (K, 198)

ORDER: UMBELLALES
Family: Araliaceae

Hedera helix L. (English ivy) 50

Family: Umbelliferae

Ammi majus L. (ammi) (ACS, 505; K, 373)

Subclass: Asteridae
ORDER: GENTIANALES
Family: Loganiaceae

Strychnos nux-vomica L. (strychnine tree) (A, 20; Q, 713)

Family: Gentianaceae

Centaurium umbellatum Gilib. (centaury, mountain pink) 51

Family: Apocynaceae

Adenium coetanium Stapf. (mock azalea, desert rose) ref: Paul Weissich
Allamanda spp. (allamanda) 52
Alstonia scholaris (L.) R. Br. (devil tree, dita) (Q, 720)
Catharanthus roseus (L.) G. Don (periwinkle) 53
Cerbera manghas L. (cerbera, reva) 54
C. tanghin Hook. (ordeal bean) (A, 32; Q, 727; N, 692)

Ervatamia divaricata (L.) Burkhill and E. orientalis (R. Br.) Bomin. (crape jasmine) (H, 129; K, 264)
Nerium indicum Miller and N. oleander L. (oleander) 24
Plumeria spp. (plumeria, frangipani) 54

Strophanthus spp. (strophanthus) (Q, 737)
Thevetia peruviana (Pers.) K. Schum. and T. thevetioides (H.B.K.) K. Schum. (be-still tree, yellow oleander)
                                                Family: Asclepiadaceae
Asclepias curassavica L. (milkweed) (K, 267; Q, 742)
Calotropis gigantea (L.) R. Br. (giant crownflower) 56
Calotropis procera (Ait.) R. Br. (crownflower) 56
Cryptostegia grandiflora (Roxb.) Π. Br. (pink allamanda) (H, 133; K, 270; Q, 748)

                                        ORDER: POLEMONIALES
                                            Family: Solanaceae
Capsicum spp. (red pepper, chili pepper) (Q, 835)
Cestrum spp. (cestrum, fragrance of the night) 57
Datura arborea L. and D. candida (Pers.) Pasq. (angel's trumpet) 27
D. metel L. (garden datura) 30
D. Stramonium L. (jimson weed, Jamestown weed, kikania haole, la'au-hano) 30
Lycopersicon esculentum Mill. (tomato) 72
Nicotiana spp. (tobacco) 57
Physalis peruviana L. (ground cherry, poha) 72
Solandra grandiflora Sw. (silvercup) 58
Solandra harwegii N.E. Br. (cup of gold) 53
Solanum spp. 59,73
                                        Family: Convolvulaceae
Argyreia nervosa (Burm.f.) Boj. (small wood rose) (Q, 754)
Ipomoea spp. (morning glories, moonflower, sweet potato) (K, 271; H, 133)
Merremia peltata (L.) Merr. (merremia) (Q, 763)
Operculina tuberosa (L.) Meisn. and O. turpethum (L.) Manso (wood rose) (Q, 766)
                                        ORDER: LAMIALES
                                            Family: Verbenaceae
Duranta repens L. (golden dewdrop) (H, 134; K, 295; Q, 792)
Gmelina elliptica J.E. Smith (Q, 793)
Lantana camara L. (lantana) 62
Stachytarpheta jamaicensis (L.) Vahl (Jamaica vervain, owi, oi) (Q, 801)
Vitex parviflora Juss. (vitex) (Q, 806)
                                        ORDER: PLANTAGINALES
                                            Family: Plantaginaceae
Plantago major L. (common plantain, lau-kahi) (Q, 894)
                                        ORDER: SCROPHULARIALES
                                            Family: Oleaceae
Jasminum sambac (L.) Ait. (Arabian jasmine, pikake) (Q, 706)
Ligustrum spp. (privet) (K, 263)
                                        Family: Scrophulariaceae
Digitalis purpurea L. (foxglove) 54
                                        ORDER: CAMPANULALES
                                            Family: Campanulaceae
Laurentia longiflora (L.) Endl. (star of Bethlehem) 27
Lobelia spp. (lobelia, cardinal flower) (K, 390)
                                        ORDER: RUBIALES
                                            Family: Rubiaceae
Gardenia augusta (L.) Merr. (gardenia) (Q, 904)
                                        ORDER: DIPSACALES
                                            Family: Caprifoliaceae
Sambucus mexicana Presl. (elderberry) 80

ORDER: ASTERALES
Family: Compositae (Asteraceae)

Eupatorium adenophorum Spreng. (snakeroot, pā-makani haole) 64
Rudbeckia spp. (golden glow, coneflower, thimbleweed) (K, 422)
Senecio spp. (groundsel, senecio, stinking willie) (ACS, 473; K, 425)

Xanthium saccharatum Wallr. (cocklebur) (ACS, 501; K, 440)

CLASS: MONOCOTYLEDONAE
Subclass: Commelinidae
ORDER: CYPERALES
Family: Gramineae (Poaceae)

Sorghum spp. (sorghum, Johnson grass, Sudan grass) (K, 26; 488; Q, 88)

Subclass: Arecidae
ORDER: ARECALES
Family: Palmae (Arecaceae)

Areca catechu L. (betel nut) (Q, 121; H, 51)
Arenga pinnata (Wurmb.) Merr. (sugar palm) (K,35)
Caryota mitis Lour. (fishtail palm) (K, 35)
C. urens L. (fishtail palm, wine palm, toddy palm) (K, 35)

ORDER: ARALES
Family: Araceae

Acorus calamus L. (sweet flag) 64
Aglaonema spp. 64
Alocasia spp. 64,74
Amorphophallus spp. 64
Caladium spp. (caladium) 64
Colocasia spp. (taro, kalo) 64, 74.
Dieffenbachia spp. (dumbcane) 30
Philodendron spp. (philodendron) 64
Pistia stratiotes L. (water lettuce) 64
Zantedeschia spp. (calla lily) 64

Subclass: Liliidae
ORDER: LILIALES
Family: Liliaceae

Allium cepa L. (onion), A. sativum L. (garlic) and A. schoenoprasm L. (chives) 75
Convallaria majallis L. (lily of the valley) (H, 44; K, 451)
Gloriosa rothschildiana O'Brien and G. superba L. (gloriosa lily) 66
Nolina recurvata (Lem.) Engl. (sacahuista, beargrass) (K, 453)
Ornithogalum thyrsoides Jacq. and O. umbellatum L. (star of Bethlehem) (H, 46; K, 456)

Family: Amaryllidaceae

Crinum asiaticum L. (spider lily) (Q, 171)
Eurycles amboinensis (L.) Lindl. (Brisbane lily) (Q, 174)
Narcissus spp. (narcissus, jonquil, daffodil) (K, 468)
Pancratium littorale Jacq. (spider lily) (Q, 174)
Zephyranthes atamasco (L.) Herb. (wind flower) (K, 469)

Family: Dioscoreaceae

Dioscorea bulbifera L. (yam, air potato, hoi) 75

APPENDIX B: LIST OF ALTERNATE LATIN NAMES

The Latin names used in this book are those listed as preferred names in Saint John: *List of Flowering Plants in Hawaii.* When you are reading other books a plant may be listed under any of several Latin names. To help you know when two names refer to the same plant the following list is provided.

Alternate name	Name listed in this book
Abrus luteoseminalis St. John	A. precatorius var. luteoseminalis St. John 13
Achras mammosa l .	Calocarpum sapota 90
Aglaia domestica (Correa) Pellegrin	Lansium domesticum 91
Allamanda hendersonii Bull	A. cathartica var. hendersonii (Bull) Regel 52
Aliamanda schotii Pohl	A. cathartica var. Schotii (Pohl) Bailey and Rafill 52
Amaryllis atamasco L.	Zephyranthes atamasco 93
Amygdalus communis L.	Prunus dulcis (Mill.) D. A. Webb 77
Amygdalus persica L.	Prunus persica (L.) Batsch. 77
Anagallis coerulea Schreb.	A. arvensis var. coerulea (Schreb.) Gren. and Godr. 89
Andropogon sorghum	Sorghum spp. (It has been segregrated into several species of Sorghum.) 93
Anemone japonica Sieb. & Zucc.	A. hupehensis 33
Arenga saccharifera Labill.	A. pinnata 93
Argemone alba var. glauca Prain	A. glauca 11
Argemone mexicana Hbd. (non L.)	A. glauca 11
Argyreia speciosa (L.f) Sweet	A. nervosa 92
Arum bicolor Ait.	Caladium bicolor (Ait.) Vent. 65
Arum cucullatum Lour.	Alocasia cucullata (Lour.) G. Don 65
Arum macrorrhizon L.	Alocasia macrorrhiza (L.) Sweet 65
Arum seguine Jacq.	Dieffenbachia seguine (Jacq.) Schott 30
Asclepias gigantea L.	Calotropis gigantea 56
Asclepias procera Ait.	Calotropis procera 56
Averrhoa acida L.	Phyllanthus acidus 78
Azalea indica L.	Rhododendron indicum 38
Barringtonia speciosa J.R. & G. Forst.	B. asiatica 89
Beaucarnea recurvata Lem.	Nolina recurvata 93
Boerhavia tetrandra Forst. f.	B. diffusa var. tetrandra (Forst. f.) Heimerl 89
Brugmansia arborea (L.) Steud.	Datura arborea 27
Brugmansia candida Pers.	Datura candida 27
Caladium esculentum (L.) Vent.	Colocasia esculenta 65, 74
Calla nitida Jack	Agloanema nitidum (Jack) Kunth 64
Calla picta Roxb.	Aglaonema pictum (Roxb.) Kunth 64
Centaurium minus Moench	C. umbellatum 51
Cerbera peruviana Pers.	Thevetia peruviana 24
Cerbera thevetioides HBK	Thevetia thevetioides 24
Cicca distichus L.	Phyllanthus acidus 78
Cleome gynandra L.	Gynandropsis gynandra 89
Cleome pentaphylla L.	Gynandropsis gynandra 89
Convolvulus spp. (in part)	Ipomoea spp. (in part) 92
Convolvulus nervosus Burm. f.	Argyreia nervosa 92
Convolvulus peltatus L.	Merremia peltata 92
Convolvulus speciosus L. f.	Argyreia nervosa 92

Plumbago rosea L.	P. indica L. 89
Poinciana gilliesii Hook.	Caesalpinia gilliesii 90
Poinciana pulcherrima L.	Caesalpinia pulcherrima 90
Poinsettia pulcherrima (Willd.) R. Grah.	Euphorbia pulcherrima 45
Pueraria thunbergiana (S. & Z.) Benth.	P. lobata 90
Quamoclit pennata (Desr.) Boj.	Ipomoea quamoclit L. 92
Rhamnus jujuba L.	Zizyphus mauritiana Lam. 91
Saguerus pinnata Wurmb.	Arenga pinnata 93
Sambucus bipinnata Schlecht. & Cham.	S. mexicana 80
Schismatoglottis crispa Pitcher & Manda	Aglaonema crispum (Pitcher & Manda)
	D. H. Nicholson 30
Scindapsus haenkei Presl.	Aglaonema haenkei (Presl.) Schott 30
Sideroxylon sapota Jacq.	Calocarpum sapota 90
Sinapis juncea L.	Brassica juncea (L.) Czernj. & Coss. 68
Sinapis pekinensis Lour.	Brassica pekinensis (Lour.) Rupr. 68
Solandra nitida Zucc.	S. hartwegii 58
Sorghum vulgare L.	Segregated into several spp. of Sorghum 93
Spartium scoparium L.	Cytisus scoparius 90
Stilago bunius L.	Antidesma bunius 91
Stylurus banksii (R. Br. in Knight) Deg.	Grevillea banksii 43
Syzygium cuminii (L.) Skeels	Eugenia cuminii 90
Syzygium jambos (L.) Alston.	Eugenia jambos 90
Tabernaemontana coronaria (Jacq.) Willd.	Ervatamia divaricata 92
Tabernaemontana divaricata R. Br.	Ervatamia divaricata 92
Tabernaemontana orientalis R. Br.	Ervatamia orientalis 92
Tacsonia manicata Juss.	Passiflora manicata (Juss.) Pers. 75
Tacsonia molissima HBK	Passiflora molissima (HBK) Bailey 75
Tacsonia sanguinea (Sm.) DC	Passiflora vitifolia HBK 75
Tacsonia van-voxemii Lemaire	Passiflora antioquiensis Karst. 75
Tanghinia venenifera Poir.	Cerbera tanghin Hook. 54
Thevetia aurantiaca	T. peruviana forma aurantiaca D. 24
Thevetia yccotli A. DC	T. thevetioides 24
Varneria augusta L.	Gardenia augusta 92
Verbena jamaicensis L.	Stachytarpheta jamaicensis 92
Virburnum macrophyllum Rhunb.	Hydrangea macrophylla 39
Vinca rosea L.	Catharanthus roseus 53
Xanthium strumarium L.	X. saccharatum 93
Zizyphus jujuba L.	Zizyphus mauritiana 91

APPENDIX C: GLOSSARY

alternate: arranged singly along a stem (one leaf to a node, for example)
berry: a fleshy fruit with more than one seed.
bipinnate: twice pinnate

bract: a leaf associated with a flower or inflorescence.
calyx: the outer whorl of floral leaves; the sepals taken collectively
capsule: a fruit with more than one locule, opening on ripening
carcinogenic: cancer-causing
cardiac: referring to the heart
cathartic: a substance which causes diarrhea (cf. purgative and laxative)
caustic: capable of destroying tissue
cleft: deeply lobed with indentations half way or more to the midrib

coma: profound unconsciousness
compound leaf: a leaf with more than one blade

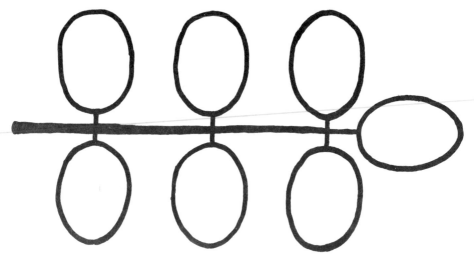

conjunctivitis: inflammation of the mucous membrane of the eye
convulsions: severe, involuntary muscular contractions, usually with unconscious-
             ness
cordate: heart-shaped with the point away from the locus of attachment

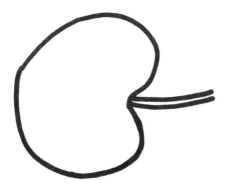

corm: a short, thick, fleshy stem with at least part underground (Taro has corms.)
corolla: the inner whorl of floral leaves; the petals taken collectively
corymb: a flattened cluster of flowers or fruits

crenate: toothed with rounded points (referring to leaf margins)

cyanogenic: capable of producing hydrocyanic acid
cyanophoric: with cyanogenic substances. "cyanogenic" usually refers of a chemi-
          cal, while "cyanophoric" refers to the plants.
dehydration: loss of water
delirium: confused or delusional disorientation of mental processes
dentate: ` toothed (referring to leaf margins)

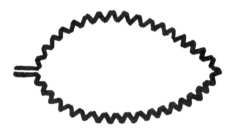

dermatitis: inflammation of the skin
diastole: the period of a heartbeat in which the heart muscles relax
diplopia: inability to coordinate the eyes; double vision
diuretic: causing increased flow of the urine.
drupe: a fleshy fruit with one seed.
edema: accumulation of fluids in cells of any tissue, causing swelling
emetic: causing vomiting (emesis)
endemic: native to an area and found nowhere else. (cf. indigenous)
enzyme: a biological catalyst. Enzymes are all proteins.
erythrocyte: red blood corpuscle
euphoria: a feeling of well-being or elation
gastroenteritis: inflammation of the stomach and intestinal tract. Symptoms are
             usually vomiting and diarrhea.
gastrointestional: referring to the stomach and intestinal tract
habitat: the place or environment in which a plant is living
head: in plants, a cluster of flowers without stalks, arising from a single point

hemolytic: causing breakdown of the red blood corpuscles (hemolysis)
herbaceous: having only non-woody tissue (herb)
hypertensive: causing high blood pressure
hypoglycemia: low bood sugar. (hypoglycemic)
indigenous: native to a place; not introduced by man (cf. endemic)
inflorescence: any naturally occurring cluster of flowers or fruit
internode: the space on a stem between successive nodes
lanceolate (leaf shape): several times as long as wide

lateral: emerging from the side of a stem (not the tip or base)
latex: milky sap
laxative: causing increased, but normal bowel movements (cf. purgative and
          cathartic)
LD$_{50}$: a dosage which causes half of a group of experimental animals to die
locule: the cavity of a carpel of a fruit. The spaces in a tomato are locules.
lobe: (of a leaf or flower): a projection on a leaf or flower

mucosa, mucous membrane: the membrane lining the mouth, throat, gastorintesti-
nal tract and some other parts of the body. The mucous membrane secretes fluids
which keep it always moist.

narcotic: originally this word meant "causing sleep, usually with reduction of pain."
The medical term has been confused with the legal term. Legally a narcotic is any
substance controlled by the narcotics laws, whether or not it has any truly narcotic
effects. (narcosis)

netted venation: having vascular tissue (veins) interconnected

neurological: referring to the nerves or the nervous system

nodes: the regularly spaced joints on a stem, where the leaves are normally attached
         to the stem

nut: a single-seeded fruit with a fibrous, dry husk

oblong (leaf shape): having a more or less rectangular shape

opposite (leaf arrangement): arranged in pairs (two to a node) along a stem

orbicular (leaf shape): circular in outline

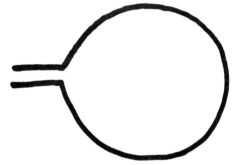

oval (leaf shape): broadly elliptic

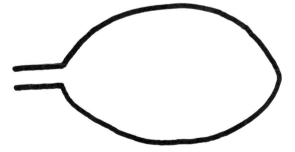

ovate (leaf shape): egg-shaped, with the large end near the petiole

ovoid: egg-shaped and solid

palmate: arising from a single point

panicle: an inflorescence with a long central stalk from which side branches arise, at
        least one of which has more than one flower

pantropic: occurring throughout the tropics
parallel venation: having vascular tissue (veins) in rows and not interconnected (or very weakly interconnected)
pedical: a stalk of a flower
pendulous: limply suspended
perennial: living more than one year
petiole: a stalk of a leaf
pinnate (of leaves): arising from a central stalk or vein

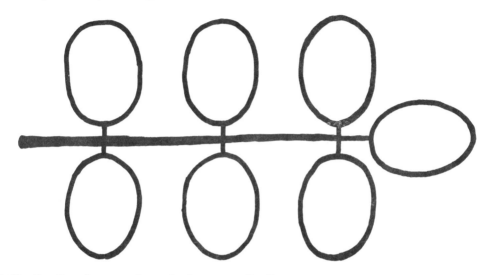

pistil: the female or seed-producing part of a flower
pod: a legume or fruit of the family Leguminosae. It has a single row of seeds in an enclosing ovary, which breaks open along two sutures.
purgative: a substance which causes diarrhea. In this book purgative and cathartic are cathartic are synonyms. Laxative, in contrast, refers to a substance which causes increased but normal bowel movements
raceme: an inflorescence with a central stalk from which arise single, stalked flowers

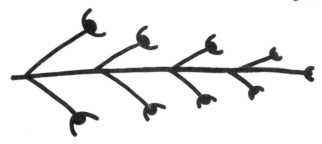

raphides: needle-like crystals of calcium oxalate
reflexed: abruptly turned back on itself
retina: the light-sensitive tissue of the eye
salivation: flow of saliva; "atering of the mouth"
sedative: a substance which calms or quiets a person
soporific: a substance which puts a person to sleep

spike: an inflorescence with a central stalk from which arise flowers without stalks

stamen: the male, or pollen-producing, part of a flower

style (of a flower): stalk of a pistil (female part) of a flower. At the end of the style
                      isthe stigma, which accepts the pollen for fertilization.

subtend: to be situated below or at the base of an organ

succulent: having fleshy or juicy tissue

suture (in botany): a seam or line in a fruit, along which the fruit typically breaks
                     open on ripening

systole: the contraction of the heart which forces blood into the arteries (systolic)

tendril: a part of a leaf or stem which twines about other objects for support

terminal: at the tips of stems

teratogenic: causing deformaties of a fetus or embryo

tuber: a fleshy, underground stem. A potato is a tuber.

umbel: an inflorescence in which stalked flowers arise from a single point

variegated: having spots or patches of more than one color or shade

venation: the arrangement of vascular tissue (veins) in a leaf

vertigo: dizziness

vesicant: causing blistering

REFERENCES

Abbrev.
used in
text

Ad   Adams, C. Dennis: *The Blue Mahoe and Other Bush;* Sangsters Bookstores Ltd. (95 Harbour St. Kingston, Jamaica) 1971

ACS   *American Chemical Society Symposium on Natural Food Toxicants;* J. Agr. & Food Chem 17: 413-538. 1969

A   Arnold, Harry L. Sr.: *Poisonous Plants of Hawaii* Tuttle (Tokyo) 1944

Ar   Arnold, Harry L. Jr.: Dermatitis Due to the Blossom of *Grevillea Banksii; Arch. Dermatology and syphiology 45;* 1037-1051. 1942

—   Arnold, Harry L. Jr.; personal communication

CU   Brecher, et al: *The Consumers Union Report: Licit and Illicit Drugs;* Consumers Union (Mt. Vernon, N.Y.) 1972

—   Chittenden, R.F., former Director of the Poison Control Information Center, Honolulu, HI; personal communication

Cr   Cronquist, Arthur: *The Evolution and Classification of Flowering Plants;* Houghton-Mifflin Co. (Boston) 1968

D1   Degener, Otto and Isa Degener: *Flora Hawaiiensis;* publ. by the authors

D2   Degener, Otto: *Plants of the Hawaii National Park;* Edwards Litho (Ann Arbor, Mich.) 1945

Dr   Dreisbach, Robert: *Handbook of Poisoning,* Eighth Edition; Lange Medical Publications (Los Altos, CA) 1974

Ga   Gardner, Eldon: *Principles of Genetics,* Fourth Edition; John Wiley & Sons (New York) 1971

H   Hardin, James and Jay Arena: *Human Poisoning from Native and Introduced Plants,* Second Edition; Duke University Press (Durham, N.C.) 1974

K   Kingsbury, John: *Poisonous Plants of the United States and Canada;* Prentice-Hall (Englewood Cliffs, N.J.) 1964

N   Neal, Marie C.: *In Gardens of Hawaii;* Bishop Museum Press (Honolulu, HI) 1965

O   Oakes, A.J. and J.O. Butcher: *Poisonous and Injurious Plants of the U.S. Virgin Islands;* U.S.D.A. Miscel. Publ. 882 (Washington, D.C.) 1962

PT   Polson, C.J. and R.N. Tattersall: *Clinical Toxicology* Lippencott (Philadelphia) 1969

Q   Quisumbing, Eduardo: *Medicinal Plants of the Philippines;* Bureau of Printing Technical Bull. No. 16 (Manila) 1951

S   St. John, Harold: *List and Summary of the Flowering Plants in the Hawaiian Islands;* Pacific Tropical Gardens Memoir No. 1 (Lawai, Kauai, HI) 1973

—   Tabrah, Frank, Professor of Medicine, University of Hawaii; unpublished data and personal communication.

—   Weissich, Paul, Curator of Foster Botanical Gardens, Honolulu; personal communication